TEACHING EARLY NUMERACY TO CHILDREN WITH DEVELOPMENTAL DISABILITIES

TEACHING EARLY NUMERACY TO CHILDREN WITH DEVELOPMENTAL DISABILITIES

CORINNA F. GRINDLE

RICHARD P. HASTINGS

ROBERT J. WRIGHT

SAGE Publications Ltd
1 Oliver's Yard
55 City Road
London EC1Y 1SP

CORWIN
A SAGE company
2455 Teller Road
Thousand Oaks, California 91320
(0800)233-9936
www.corwin.com

SAGE Publications India Pvt Ltd
B 1/I 1 Mohan Cooperative Industrial Area
Mathura Road
New Delhi 110 044

SAGE Publications Asia-Pacific Pte Ltd
3 Church Street
#10-04 Samsung Hub
Singapore 049483

Editor: James Clark
Assistant editor: Diana Alves
Assistant editor, digital: Sunita Patel
Production editor: Nicola Carrier
Copyeditor: Jane Fricker
Proofreader: Sharon Cawood
Indexer: Silvia Benvenuto
Marketing manager: Dilhara Attygalle
Cover design: Wendy Scott
Typeset by: C&M Digitals (P) Ltd, Chennai, India
Printed in the UK

© Corinna F. Grindle, Richard P. Hastings and Robert J. Wright 2021

First published 2021

Library of Congress Control Number: 2020934664

British Library Cataloguing in Publication data

A catalogue record for this book is available from the British Library

ISBN 978-1-5264-8754-4
ISBN 978-1-5264-8753-7 (pbk)

At SAGE we take sustainability seriously. Most of our products are printed in the UK using responsibly sourced papers and boards. When we print overseas we ensure sustainable papers are used as measured by the PREPS grading system. We undertake an annual audit to monitor our sustainability.

To Paul, Milo and Holly

To Stephanie

To Ann Stafford

The Mathematics Recovery book series

Teaching Early Numeracy to Children with Developmental Disabilities is the seventh book in the Mathematics Recovery series. The books in this series address the teaching of early number, whole number arithmetic and fractions in primary, elementary and secondary education. These books provide practical help to enable schools and teachers to give equal status to numeracy intervention and classroom instruction. The authors are internationally recognized as leaders in this field and draw on considerable practical experience of delivering professional learning programs, training courses and materials.

The other Mathematics Recovery books are:

Early Numeracy: Assessment for Teaching and Intervention, 2nd edition, Robert J. Wright, Jim Martland and Ann K. Stafford, 2006. *Early Numeracy* demonstrates how to assess students' mathematical knowledge, skills and strategies in addition, subtraction, multiplication and division.

Teaching Number: Advancing Children's Skills and Strategies, 2nd edition, Robert J. Wright, Jim Martland, Ann K. Stafford and Garry Stanger, 2006. *Teaching Number* sets out in detail nine principles which guide the teaching, together with 180 practical, exemplar teaching procedures to advance children to more sophisticated strategies for solving arithmetic problems.

Developing Number Knowledge: Assessment, Teaching and Intervention with 7–11 Year-Olds, Robert J. Wright, David Ellemor-Collins and Pamela Tabor, 2012. *Developing Number Knowledge* provides more advanced knowledge and resources for teachers working with older students.

Teaching Number in the Classroom with 4–8 Year-Olds, 2nd edition, Robert J. Wright, Garry Stanger, Ann K. Stafford and Jim Martland, 2014. *Teaching Number in the Classroom* shows how to extend the work of assessment and intervention with individual and small groups to working with whole classes.

Developing Fractions Knowledge, Amy J. Hackenberg, Anderson Norton and Robert J. Wright, 2016. *Developing Fractions Knowledge* provides a detailed progressive approach to assessment and instruction related to students' learning of fractions.

The Learning Framework in Number: Pedagogical Tools for Assessment and Instruction, Robert J. Wright and David Ellemor-Collins, 2018. This book presents a learning framework across the whole K to 5 range, and provides three sets of pedagogical tools for the framework – assessment schedules, models of learning progressions and teaching charts. These tools enable detailed assessment and profiling of children's whole number **arithmetic knowledge**, and the development of specific instructional programs.

Numeracy for All Learners: Teaching Mathematics to Students with Special Needs, Pamela D. Tabor, Dawn Dibley, Amy J. Hackenberg, Anderson Norton. **Forthcoming 2021.** This eighth book in the series explores how the pedagogical content knowledge discussed in the previous books in the series can be utilized by teachers of students with a wide range of special educational needs.

Contents

About the authors

Corinna F. Grindle is an associate professor at the Centre for Educational Development Appraisal and Research (CEDAR), University of Warwick, UK. Corinna obtained her undergraduate degree at the University of Warwick, and her PhD at the University of Southampton, in 2004. She has over 25 years' experience working with children and adults with autism and related developmental disabilities. Corinna has taught university courses for teachers and specialists regarding autism, developmental disabilities, curriculum design and effective instruction. She has been invited to present at national and international conferences regarding educational, behavioral and communicative issues relating to children and young people with developmental disabilities. Corinna's research interests include early intervention, challenging behavior, and fostering academic learning for students with moderate and severe developmental disabilities. Her research has been published in several peer-reviewed journals including the *Journal of Autism and Developmental Disabilities* and *Research in Developmental Disabilities*.

Richard P. Hastings is a Professor of Psychology and Education in the Centre for Educational Development Appraisal and Research at the University of Warwick, UK, and Monash Warwick Professor in the Centre for Developmental Psychiatry and Psychology at Monash University, Australia. Richard is an internationally leading researcher focused on children and adults with developmental disabilities (especially intellectual disability and/or autism) and their families, and one of the highest cited special education researchers internationally. His research interests include mental health and well-being in schools, and developing and testing academic interventions for children with special educational needs in both mainstream and special education settings.

Robert J. (Bob) Wright holds Bachelor's and Master's degrees in mathematics from the University of Queensland (Australia) and a doctoral degree in mathematics education from the University of Georgia. He is an adjunct professor in mathematics education at Southern Cross University in New South Wales. Bob is an internationally recognized leader in assessment and instruction relating to children's early arithmetical knowledge and strategies, publishing six books, and many articles and papers in this field. His work over the last 25 years has included the development of the **Mathematics Recovery** program, which focuses on providing specialist training for teachers to advance the numeracy levels of young children assessed as low-attainers. In Australia and New Zealand, Ireland, the

UK, the USA, Canada, Mexico, South Africa and elsewhere, this program has been implemented widely, and applied extensively to classroom teaching and to average and able learners as well as low-attainers. Bob has conducted several research projects funded by the Australian Research Council, including the most recent project focusing on assessment and intervention in the early arithmetical learning of low-attaining 8- to 10-year-olds.

About the Lesson Plans and Online Resources

The lesson plans and other online resources can be accessed at
https://study.sagepub.com/corwin/grindle using the access code printed in the inside
cover of this book.

Lesson plans

Teaching Early Numeracy to Children with Developmental Disabilities is supported by a comprehensive set of **over 90** lesson plans for you to download, print and use in the classroom.
These have been adapted from classic 'green book' Mathematics Recovery material for specific use with children with developmental disabilities. The lesson plans are split into three
main categories covering the emergent, perceptual and figurative phases of mathematical
development. Each phase of mathematical development includes five or six key topics
that fall into one of the following three strands: number words and numerals, counting
and grouping. All lesson plans follow the same structure. The *materials* section describes
the teaching resources required to deliver a lesson. The *teaching procedure* section summarizes some recommendations for how best to teach a skill. The *generalization plan* section
provides examples of teaching strategies for encouraging maintenance and generalization.
The *help that may be provided* section, provides examples of different teaching supports
that may be helpful if a student is struggling to learn a skill. Finally, *the mastery criterion*
section specifies the number of independent correct responses required over a number of
days for a skill to be considered mastered (learned). Prerequisite skill lesson plans also
provide suggestions for how to teach crucial readiness skills such as attending, imitation
and matching.

Additional online resources

Alongside the lesson plans, this book offers a range of additional downloadable resources
These include:

Practical numeracy resources

A selection of practical resources to be downloaded and printed and used in teaching, including:

- Numeral cards covering different number ranges
- Numeral sequences coverings different number ranges
- Five-frame and ten-frame grids
- Pairs pattern cards
- Colored dots in different quantities

Teacher resources

A range of data sheets and related documents to support teachers, including:

- Reinforcer sampling letter for parents
- Reinforcer inventory
- Preference assessment data sheets
- Reinforcer sampling instructions and materials
- Cold probe data sheets
- Skills trackers (for emergent, figurative and perceptual skills)
- Generalization data sheet

Assessment resources

Assessment checklists to probe emergent, perceptual and figurative skills. Files here include:

- List and description of teaching resources
- Emergent probe checklist
- Perceptual probe checklist
- Figurative probe sheet

Acknowledgments

The lesson plans that accompany this book are based on original material from the Mathematics Recovery green book, *Teaching Number: Advancing Children's Skills and Strategies*, 2nd edition by Robert J. Wright, James Martland, Ann K. Stafford and Gary Stanger (2006) and adapted by Corinna Grindle, Magdalena Apanasionok, Beverley Ann Jones and Pagona Tzanakaki. The prerequisite skills lesson plans were developed by Magdalena Apanasionok, Beverley Ann Jones., Corinna Grindle and Kayleigh Caldwell.

The authors wish to thank all the teachers and students who have participated in and contributed to the development of *Teaching Early Numeracy to Children with Developmental Disabilities*. In particular, we would like to thank Lara Latham, Leanne Maguire and Darragh Staunton from Calthorpe Academy in the UK. Your feedback on the content of the lesson plans and data sheets has been gratefully received. We also wish to express our gratitude and appreciation to Pagona Tzanakaki and Magdalena Apanasionok, two outstanding PhD students who greatly contributed to the development of the program. We acknowledge the assistance from the Sharland Foundation Developmental Disabilities ABA Research and Impact Network (SF-DDARIN) in funding support in the form of Research Assistant time to develop the lesson plans. We would also like to thank especially Beverley Ann Jones for her excellent contributions to all the lesson plans and Kayleigh Caldwell for her helpful input in developing the prerequisite skills lesson plans.

1

Introduction

Sheila's story

Sheila is 6 years old and has a diagnosis of autism. She goes to an autism unit that is attached to a mainstream school. Although Sheila is able to speak in full sentences, her teachers report that she is performing well below her chronological age in numeracy. She does not yet name numerals up to 10 consistently and is not able to count objects with correspondence. She gets very easily frustrated when she is presented with numeracy tasks and usually responds immediately by throwing herself under the table and screaming loudly. Sheila's teachers are despairing and cannot see how they are ever going to be able to teach her any numeracy skills. With each passing week she is getting further and further behind her classmates. Sheila's teachers ask for help. They receive some training on how to deliver a specialist numeracy program designed specifically for children with autism and other children with a developmental disability. They learn how to choose numeracy tasks to teach that are matched to Sheila's level of ability and they learn how to provide help systematically in a way that ensures that Sheila is more successful with her learning and that she gradually relies less and less on receiving help until she is answering quickly and confidently. Sheila's teachers also discover how to motivate Sheila better so that she is much more willing to engage in her numeracy work.

Sheila receives this early intervention numeracy program in short bursts of teaching daily over a period of 20 weeks. Now Sheila is able to count to 30 and can easily name numerals up to 20. She is able to arrange collections of objects into equal groups (e.g., putting 10 plastic teddy bears into five groups of two) and describe the groups. Although Sheila's parents have not received training on the program, they are thrilled to notice that Sheila is using her newly learnt skills in the home. She now plays with her younger brother

(Continued)

and organizes tea parties where she shares out and counts cups and saucers that she places in front of her teddy bears. When her parents tell her to 'take just three sweets', she knows exactly what they mean and takes the correct amount. After 20 weeks, Sheila's teacher in the autism unit arranges a meeting with the first-grade teacher in the main-stream part of the school. They agree that Sheila is now at the level in numeracy at which she should be able to attend mathematics lessons with her same-aged neurotypical peers. Sheila is offered a little bit of extra support to help get her used to learning in a group, but by the end of the school year Sheila is going into the mainstream school for all of her mathematics lessons, is able to work independently of specialist support, and is no longer considered to be 'at risk' for her numeracy skill development. One year later, Sheila has moved to a new school. She is assessed again to see how well she is doing. Sheila is still able to access typical mathematics teaching in a mainstream school setting and has main-tained all of the gains that she made following the 20-week program.

David's story

David is 15 years old and goes to a special school for children with severe developmental disabilities. David also has a diagnosis of autism and very little speech. He mostly com-municates using just one- or two-word phrases. Like many young people with a severe autism diagnosis, David frequently engages in self-stimulatory behavior. For David, he makes very loud noises, rocks his body back and forth or flaps his hands to the side of his face. Throughout all his school years, David engaged in this self-stimulatory behavior for much of the school day, including when his teachers were attempting to teach him new skills. This had had a deleterious effect on his ability to attend to his teachers and to learn use-ful skills. David had always struggled to be motivated to do numeracy work and could not say the number word sequence from 1 to 10. Nor could he identify numerals up to five consistently. David did not like to do numeracy work, or indeed any other schoolwork, and would protest loudly or bang on the table whenever teaching materials were presented to him. Sometimes he would tip his chair up and run around the classroom.

David has now been on a specialist numeracy program, developed for children and adolescents with developmental disabilities, for one year. When David is asked to come over to start his numeracy work, he immediately stops engaging in any self-stimulatory behavior that he may have been doing previously. He hurries over to his table and sits down with a smile and a laugh, ready to learn. If his teacher is too slow with getting ready to teach, David hands over his teaching folder to prompt his teacher to start. He is fully engaged and smiling while he works, rarely engages in self-stimulatory behavior during teaching sessions and likes to give his teacher a high-five when he knows he has answered correctly. David is now able to say the number word sequence up to 10 forwards and backwards and can count objects with one-to-one correspondence in a variety of different situations, including outside of teaching sessions. He is able to take a specified number of objects from a larger group of objects and can also copy and count sequences of sounds. The teachers are amazed that he has finally been able to learn these skills during his later school years as they had thought previously that this skill acquisition was probably beyond his abilities. David's teachers report that he seems really proud of his achievements during his numeracy lessons and that they are proud of him too.

The functional benefits of learning these skills for David have been considerable. He is able to shop more independently now by selecting the correct number of items to put into a basket. He can now also count using his fingers, a skill that is more easily transferred to a range of community contexts where he does not have to rely on having teaching resources like counters available to help him count. In cooking lessons, David is able to count out the correct number of cups of flour to put into a bowl when he is making cakes. David never complains about doing his numeracy lessons anymore. His teachers report that his willingness to participate in schoolwork, and his ability to remain focused during teaching, have extended to all other areas of the curriculum as well.

Although Sheila and David's names have been changed to protect their anonymity, their stories are real accounts of two very different journeys taken following the introduction of a specialist numeracy program that has been developed specifically to help children and young people with a developmental disability. This book is all about young people like Sheila and David who have significant disabilities and may never have been taught numeracy skills or whose teachers have struggled to teach them these skills. The book is about an approach that helps to make sure that as many young people as possible get a good early start with their numeracy skills (like Sheila), or get the chance to catch up when they are older like David. Of course, any teacher, any parent, or any other professional would want to make sure that young people like Sheila and David get the most that they can from education. However, it is important to remember that access to education is also a human right (UN Convention on the Rights of the Child [UNCRC], 1989) and is enshrined in national laws in many countries.

In the USA, 13% of all school-aged children have disabilities (Snyder et al., 2018) and in England, 14% of all students are characterized as having special educational needs (Department for Education [UK], 2019). Ever since the first law was passed 30 years ago in the USA, ensuring a free and appropriate public education for all children with disabilities (Education for All Handicapped Children Act, 1975), there has been an increasing focus in schools on developing high-quality educational programs for students with disabilities. In the USA, the Individuals with Disabilities Education Improvement Act of 2004 (IDEA, 2004) has continued to ensure this right. The No Child Left Behind Act of 2001 (NCLB, 2002) also emphasizes that schools have an obligation to provide high-quality education to all students with a disability and that all students' progress in reading, mathematics and science should be regularly assessed. The Every Student Succeeds Act (ESSA, 2015) emphasizes that evidence-based teaching practices should be used when teaching all students, including those with moderate and severe developmental disabilities.

In the UK too, under the Equality Act 2010, schools in England, Wales and Scotland are required to provide a high-quality education to all students and make reasonable adjustments for students with disabilities (Department for Education [UK], 2014). Further, following the introduction of the new Children and Families Act in 2014, statutory guidance to those providing educational services to children with special educational needs in England places a very strong emphasis on preparation for adulthood as the guiding principle for selecting outcomes for improvement (Legislation.gov.uk, 2014). Teachers are encouraged to frequently assess students' progress and set goals that are achievable yet ambitious (Department for Education [UK], 2015). Moreover, the Special Educational Needs and Disability Code of Practice for England (Department for Education and Department of Health [UK], 2015) recommends that teaching approaches should be chosen based on the available evidence.

Internationally then, education policy and guidance are clear about the importance of the inclusion of students with disabilities in education, that they need to be provided with the best quality and comprehensive educational services to be able to function as independently as possible as adults, and that evidence-based teaching strategies should be prioritized. For students with disabilities to learn general curriculum content, any instructional plan would need to have a strong focus on teaching academic domains, including mathematics.

What is special about this book?

In writing this book, we want to address the problem that there is very little detailed guidance available for teachers who want to teach number and arithmetic knowledge (numeracy) to children with a moderate or severe developmental disability. The authors consider that this book differentiates itself from other books on numeracy because it provides an extensive and detailed approach to assessment, learning and teaching that embodies evidence-based best practice. Assessment materials and detailed lesson plans are presented in a ready-to-use format, with sufficient instructions for teachers to be able to use them easily during their lessons. Thus, in writing the book, we hope to provide plenty of practical help to the teacher.

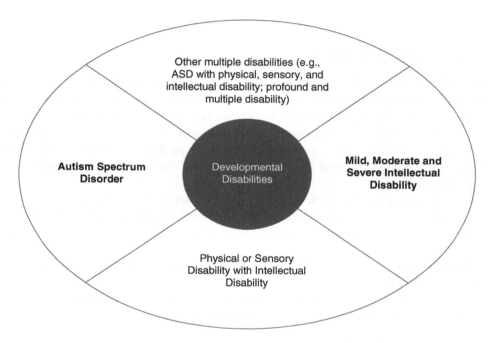

Figure 1.1 Developmental disabilities as an umbrella term to refer to students with autism spectrum disorders, intellectual disabilities and multiple disabilities

During the course of this book, we will use the general term *developmental disabilities* to describe a group of students who may have an intellectual disability or an autism spectrum disorder (ASD) or both, or sensory or physical disabilities, such as cerebral palsy or visual or hearing impairments, combined with either of these (see Figure 1.1). These are the young people in education who are like David and Sheila. These disabilities are sometimes also referred to as *low incidence* disabilities (because they affect a small proportion of all children and young people) and may be mild to severe. Intellectual disability (intellectual developmental disorder) is a condition with onset during the developmental period (before the age of 18) that includes 'both intellectual and adaptive functioning deficits in conceptual, social, and practical domains' (American Psychiatric Association, 2013). Autism spectrum disorder is a neurodevelopmental disorder characterized by deficits in social communication, social interaction and repetitive behaviors (American

Psychiatric Association, 2013). These two populations, especially in an education context, face some similar challenges, and professionals supporting them are working in a context of limited existing research literature and guidelines.

The structure of this book

This book has two main aims. The first is to equip teachers, paraprofessionals and parents with a theoretical understanding of some of the main principles of teaching and learning that underpin our approach to teaching numeracy to children with a developmental disability. The second and overarching aim of this book is to provide clear guidance on how educators can plan and implement the program so that each child can be given a positive experience in learning numeracy and achieve the best outcomes, maximizing their potential.

There are two parts to this book. The first part (Chapters 1–3) will provide the introductory context for the teaching procedures described in this book. In this first chapter, we establish the foundation for the remaining chapters by exploring the following questions:

- What are current mathematics learning outcomes for students with a developmental disability in school?
- What does the research tell us about evidence-based approaches to teaching mathematics to students with a developmental disability?

In Chapter 2, we address the question: What is Mathematics Recovery, and why might it provide a useful starting framework for teaching mathematics to children with a developmental disability? In Chapter 3, we will describe how the original Mathematics Recovery program has been adapted in this book to suit the learning needs of children with a developmental disability. We will also summarize the evidence demonstrating the benefits of using the adapted program with children with a developmental disability.

The second part (Chapters 4–8) will focus on the 'how' of teaching (the pedagogy) in teaching early numeracy to children with developmental disabilities. In Chapter 4, you will learn how to motivate your students to learn. Here, we will describe how you can identify reinforcers for the students you work with, and how to establish and use token economy reinforcement systems. In Chapter 5, we address the question: What is discrete-trial teaching, and how can it be delivered effectively? In Chapter 6, we will describe prompting and prompt fading procedures and you will also learn what to do when a child makes mistakes and how to correct errors effectively. In Chapter 7, we will describe how you can help the child to use the mathematical skills learnt in structured sessions in a variety of different settings, with different people, and across time. This chapter provides practical suggestions for including maintenance and generalization in your instruction.

In Chapter 8, the final chapter, you will be provided with an overview of the lesson plans used in this book and how they can be used. Chapter 8 will also describe how to assess the student so that you know exactly which areas should be the first to teach. You will also be provided with guidance on how to assemble a plan for instruction, including giving information on how to organize teaching sessions and how to collect data so that you can be sure that the student is learning new skills to the best of their ability.

Background to the book

What are current mathematics learning outcomes for students with a developmental disability in school?

Mathematics, of course, includes important functional skills that are used throughout a person's life. A working knowledge of mathematics underpins the capacity for independent living and being able to maintain paid employment, both of which are promoted as valued outcomes for children with disabilities (Department for Education and Department of Health [UK], 2015) and are human rights (United Nations Convention on the Rights of Persons with Disabilities [UNCRDP], 2006). Given the importance of providing a high-quality education in mathematics, the effective teaching of these skills in school is an international priority. Despite this, children with developmental disabilities appear to be at a considerable educational disadvantage when it comes to learning mathematics, and the teaching of mathematics remains a particular area of concern. For example, children with developmental disabilities (including those with mild/moderate developmental difficulties) have poor attainment in English schools. Department for Education data from 2019 show that only 33% of children aged 5–7 years with a special educational need (SEN) achieved the expected attainment levels in mathematics compared to 84% of those without SEN (Department for Education [UK], 2020). Similarly, only 21% of children with special educational needs in the UK achieved expected levels in mathematics by the time they left elementary school at the age of 11 (Department for Education [UK], 2020).

Outcomes are even poorer for children with severe developmental disabilities. National UK data also suggest that currently fewer than 7% of adults with developmental disabilities are in paid employment (Public Health England, 2015), and this is unlikely to improve if children with developmental disabilities fall further behind in mathematics at school. In the USA, a sample of 125 teachers of students with moderate and severe developmental disabilities reported that they felt unprepared when it came to teaching mathematics to this population (Lee et al., 2016).

Thus, children with a developmental disability face educational inequalities in terms of their numeracy outcomes in school and have much to gain from improved attainment in mathematics. If many children are not even acquiring the most basic mathematic skills during their school years, then these deficits will have a serious impact on vital areas of their everyday life such as being able to use money or understand quantities (Ayres et al., 2011), which in turn will impact on the quality of their life into adulthood. It is only with a full complement of educational opportunities in mathematics that children will realize their potential for increased competence for adult living, including increased opportunities in the job market and increased opportunities to live more independently. Gaining skills in mathematics curriculum content may also help to increase students' autonomy by providing them with more tools at their disposal to be able to learn valuable information and demonstrate their ability. This in turn may help to increase their feelings of self-esteem.

If we are to improve the situation by providing more guidance for educators on how to increase mathematical attainment for children with a developmental disability, it is important that we first understand the reasons why children with developmental disabilities may be underperforming in mathematics in schools, so that we can act to change them.

Why are children with a developmental disability not performing well in mathematics?

We believe that there are five reasons why children with a developmental disability may not be performing well in mathematics and these are summarized in Table 1.1.

Table 1.1 Possible reasons why children with a developmental disability are not performing well in mathematics

1.	There may be reduced opportunities to learn mathematics
2.	The structured teaching of mathematics may be underemphasized
3.	Teachers may not be confident that they know the best ways to teach mathematics
4.	Teachers may find it difficult to teach mathematical skills
5.	Teachers may find it difficult to translate research into practice

There may be reduced opportunities to learn mathematics

Students with developmental disabilities may have fewer educational opportunities to be able to learn mathematic skills compared to their neurotypical peers quite simply because mathematics appears less frequently on their weekly timetable. Some teachers believe that if a child has a developmental disability then an important focus of their education should be on teaching functional daily living skills, like cooking or making the bed, or other leisure activities like gardening or horse riding which may be an option in some special schools. In fact, Westling and Fox (2004) suggest that functional skills that can be used in daily living in the home and community should be taught on a daily basis and should always be incorporated into a child's individualized education plan (IEP). Subsequently, time that might otherwise be allocated for teaching mathematics is sometimes taken up instead with the teaching of these daily living skills or leisure activities. These skills are of course important. Nevertheless, the negative impact of not allocating sufficient time for teaching mathematics is often underestimated and this can have a major impact on a young person with a developmental disability. Prioritizing the learning of basic skills in mathematics is very important. Neurotypical students are not expected to learn such skills as being able to make a sandwich before they have mastered basic mathematical skills like being able to count objects or being able to recognize numerals. Teachers should be asking themselves if this focus on daily living skills and leisure activities is always appropriate for children with a developmental disability.

The structured teaching of mathematics may be underemphasized

Another possible explanation for children's poor performance in mathematics is that a structured approach to teaching across a comprehensive range of mathematical domains may be underemphasized. When the teaching of mathematics does occur, teachers may be sometimes driven to prioritize teaching mathematical skills that have an obvious functional aim, such as teaching children how to use money rather than focusing on a broader range of skills. While it is important to teach children skills associated with using money in community activities such as purchasing items in shops, some teachers are not quite sure about the detailed attainment steps that a child would need to learn to use confidently the skills of purchasing (which require the quite advanced prerequisite skills of addition and subtraction). Teachers then may get caught up in teaching early money skills such as naming and identifying coins and notes, which, by itself, has very little functional use in everyday community contexts.

Teachers may not be confident that they know the best ways to teach mathematics

Teachers may not always be sure about how best to teach mathematics to a child with a developmental disability, or how to properly assess children to identify the gaps in their knowledge and where they should start teaching. As mentioned previously, this supposition is borne out by a survey carried out in the USA, in which a sample of teachers of students with moderate and severe developmental disabilities reported that they felt unprepared when it came to teaching mathematics to this population (Lee et al., 2016).

Unfortunately, there are few examples of effective teaching models for teachers to follow and very little guidance regarding how to make teaching resources in mathematics suitable for a population of students with a developmental disability. In addition, there are very few curricula available for teachers to use as guidance regarding the detailed breakdown of teaching steps to take a child from learning very basic mathematical concepts such as counting and numeral recognition to more advanced skills like subtraction and division (Tzanakaki et al., 2014a). In this book, teachers will have one such tool at their disposal.

Teachers may find it difficult to teach mathematical skills

Teachers often try very hard over a long period of time to teach mathematics to students with a developmental disability in their class. Their attempts may be thwarted though by a lack of engagement or challenging behavior during the presentation of these academic tasks. This problem can, in part, be due to the lack of appropriate assessment tools available for teachers so that they are unsure how to properly assess a child in the first place to find out where exactly to start teaching. If mathematical tasks are presented that are too easy or too difficult then this can result in the child feeling frustrated and engaging in behaviors of concern such as ripping up worksheets, running out of the classroom or shouting very loudly. Students may frequently engage in these sorts of behaviors in order to escape from mathematical tasks that have already been presented or to avoid participating in any mathematical tasks at all.

Behaviors such as these are, of course, upsetting to the teacher and can be very disruptive in a classroom environment where the teacher also has to consider the impact on other learners. Naturally, the teacher may want to stop the behaviors as soon as they start occurring (perhaps by telling the child that they do not need to do their work after all) or they may decide to try to prevent them from occurring in the first place by giving the child other non-mathematical activities to do that do not trigger the challenging behavior. Alternatively, the teacher may decide that they will persist and try their very best to not 'give in', that they will endeavor to carry on teaching mathematics regardless of the challenging behavior. In reality though, even if the teacher is able to resist the challenging behavior most or some of the time, there often comes a point when the teacher decides that they just cannot continue trying to teach the child because they are just being too disruptive. So, even if a teacher concedes just every once in a while, this 'intermittent' reinforcement of the child's challenging behavior during teaching (that sometimes the child gets to avoid doing the work and sometimes they don't) means that the child will persist with the behaviors, or the behaviors will increase in frequency until the child eventually gets what they want (the teacher finally gives up presenting mathematical tasks to them). When the child gets what they want (no more mathematics work!) the challenging behavior finally stops, and this silently rewards the teacher for doing whatever they did to stop the behavior.

Teachers' lack of success with teaching mathematics to children with a developmental disability may understandably contribute to lowering their expectations and forming a belief that it is not possible to teach mathematics to such children and that many may never be able to learn basic mathematical skills. Even if a child does not engage in challenging behavior as described, they may have other learning challenges that appear to be so severe (they may be non-verbal, for example, or have considerable difficulties with auditory or visual processing) that teachers still come to the same conclusion: that it is just not going to be possible to teach them basic mathematical skills because they do not have the cognitive ability to learn them. This lowering of expectations can ultimately lead to poor outcomes in mathematics for many children and young people with a developmental disability because of the consequent reduction in learning opportunities presented to them.

The idea that only children who are quite cognitively able can learn mathematics may also originate from the theories of early childhood researchers who believed that very young children had little knowledge of, or capacity to learn, mathematical concepts. An alternative view is that competencies in mathematics may be either innate or can develop in the first years of life (e.g., Baroody et al., 2006; Clements et al., 2004; Piaget et al., 1960; Piaget & Szeminska, 1952). Certainly, the current view is that even very young children are quite capable of acquiring quite advanced skills in mathematics (Sarama & Clements, 2009). Relatedly, students with even quite significant developmental disabilities have also now been shown to be much more able to learn complex mathematical concepts that are typically taught to neurotypical children in the general curriculum than was originally thought. For example, Jimenez et al. (2008) demonstrated that students with moderate developmental disabilities were able to learn abstract problem solving using algebraic equations provided that they received highly structured teacher-based instruction with systematic prompting and repeated daily trials of instruction.

In Chapter 3, and briefly in the next section in this chapter, we discuss how it is unlikely to be the case that children, even those with quite severe developmental disabilities, are not capable of learning at least some basic mathematical skills that could have great functional value for them. This is with the proviso that teaching strategies that have been demonstrated repeatedly in peer-reviewed research to be highly effective for teaching mathematics to children and young people with a developmental disability are used. We believe that it is far better to have high expectations for all children and to try to adapt our teaching to their learning needs rather than not to try at all. If we do not at least try, then we fall into the trap of allowing our low expectations to determine the outcomes for children with a developmental disability. We strongly believe that children and young people with a developmental disability can learn and do indeed learn much more than they are often given credit for.

Teachers may find it difficult to translate research into practice

One of the most powerful factors that can affect whether or not students learn mathematical concepts is the method of instruction (i.e., 'how' they are taught). Teachers can have some influence over this by selecting and using only those teaching strategies that have been demonstrated in research to be effective (i.e., by using evidence-based teaching methods).

Nevertheless, deciphering and making sense of research so that it can be used during every-day practice in the classroom can be difficult and time-consuming for most teachers. This may result in teachers of students with developmental disabilities sometimes using teaching methods that have been shown to have little beneficial effect on student outcomes (e.g., Cook & Schirmer, 2003).

There are at least two reasons why teachers may struggle to implement evidence-based strategies in the classroom. First, it may be that teachers find it difficult and time-consuming to keep on top of the latest research evidence, and as such are unaware of the research-based strategies that exist and which have been shown to be effective. It may also be that teachers simply do not realize the importance of using evidence-based strategies and therefore do not prioritize the time to investigate them. At the beginning of the century in the USA, federal policy emphasized that teachers should apply educational practices that have been shown to have research support and that they should use 'evidence-based' methods to teach new skills to students (No Child Left Behind, 2002). This focus on evidence-based teaching strategies has also been supported by recent summaries of the literature, showing that students with developmental disabilities can be successful in learning a variety of academic content, despite their disability, provided that evidence-based practices are used (e.g., Cook et al., 2009).

Although it is important to use evidence-based practice when teaching neurotypical students (Hattie, 2009), it is absolutely essential for students with a developmental disability. As students with a developmental disability, by definition, find learning difficult, understanding and using effective evidence-based strategies becomes even more crucial. Researchers have long indicated that even children with quite mild developmental disabilities require effective evidence-based procedures to maximize their learning (e.g., Vaughn & Dammann, 2001). In reality, however, their education is sometimes based on a body of knowledge for application based on such factors as folklore (e.g., practices shared via anecdotes, word of mouth) or trial and error (e.g., Heward, 2003; Vaughn & Dammann, 2001).

The next section in this chapter provides an overview of the most relevant and up-to-date evidence-based practices for teaching mathematics to children with a developmental disability. We hope that it will provide a helpful summary, and help guide your decision making when it comes to choosing only the most effective evidence-based strategies for teaching mathematics. The next section will also help to provide a brief overview of an instructional strategy called *Systematic Instruction*. Systematic Instruction appears to have the most research support as a pedagogical method for teaching numeracy to children with a developmental disability, and forms the bedrock for the teaching methods described in this book. It will be described in more detail in Chapter 3.

What does the research tell us about evidence-based approaches to teaching mathematics to children with a developmental disability?

In the past 20 years, there has been a number of comprehensive research reviews that have focused on mathematical learning for students with a developmental disability, including some systematic reviews of the research. The purpose of a systematic review is to deliver a meticulous summary and critical appraisal of all the available primary research relevant to a particular research question (in this case: what teaching methodologies have been demonstrated by research to be effective at teaching mathematics to children with a developmental disability?). A high-quality systematic review is often thought to be one of the most important sources of evidence to guide teaching practice in schools.

Focusing on mathematical interventions for students with more significant cognitive disabilities, Browder et al. (2008) identified and reviewed 68 studies published between 1975 and 2005. Participants in the reviewed studies had diagnoses of moderate, profound, or severe intellectual disabilities or autism. Most of the 68 reviewed studies addressed the National Council of Teachers of Mathematics' (National Council of Teachers of Mathematics, 2000) components of measurement (e.g. money, purchasing and time) and 'number and operations' (calculation skills, numeral identification and counting). Just over a half (54%) of the included studies targeted 'number and operation' skills. Browder et al. (2008) reached the conclusion that the general teaching procedure associated with the best outcomes was Systematic Instruction. This is, 'teaching focused on specific, measurable responses that may either be discrete (singular) or a response chain (e.g., task analysis), and that are established through the use of defined methods of prompting and feedback based on the principles and research of Applied Behavior Analysis' (Browder, 2001, p. 95). It has several important components, including using clearly defined teaching goals (i.e., 'operationally defined' targets), using a system of prompting and prompt fading techniques, specification of error correction techniques, data collection to monitor progress, and generalization (Browder & Spooner, 2011). Additional evidence-based practices for teaching mathematics to children with a developmental disability found in this review were *in vivo* instruction (teaching real-world applications in everyday settings) and providing students with multiple opportunities to practice.

Focusing on more recent research evidence (36 studies published between 2005 and 2016), Spooner et al. (2019) drew the same conclusions as Browder et al.'s (2008) review. Additionally, Spooner et al. highlighted that even if not all the key components of Systematic Instruction are used during teaching, using just one or two of the components may be helpful. For example, they noted that mathematical procedures can be 'task analyzed' (broken down into smaller steps for teaching) and taught using systematic prompting with feedback (i.e., specific cues are provided by the teacher to increase the probability of correct responding and subsequent opportunities for positive feedback). In 2001, Butler et al. identified and reviewed 16 studies on mathematics interventions for students with mild to moderate developmental disability spanning a 10-year period (1989–98). They also concluded that Systematic Instruction was one of the most success-ful teaching methodologies for this group of children. Butler et al. also noted that frequent feedback from teachers was an extremely useful practice for them to use for children with a developmental disability.

Taken together, the findings from the systematic reviews suggest that children with a developmental disability, including those with autism, can learn mathematical skills, provided that they are taught systematically. Even quite complex mathematic skills can be taught to children with a developmental disability when prompting and prompt fad-ing procedures are used, when regular feedback is provided, when there is a detailed breakdown of difficult-to-learn skills (i.e., a task analysis is used) and when there is gener-alization of learnt skills to real-life contexts.

A summary of the key features of evidence-based practice for teaching mathematics to children with a developmental disability can be found in Table 1.2. Definitions of each of the components will be described in more detail in Chapters 3–8.

Table 1.2   Key features of evidence-based practice for teaching mathematics to children with a developmental disability

Teaching method	Definition
Systematic Instruction	Systematic Instruction incorporates the principles of Applied Behavior Analysis and has several components, including: 1. Using clearly defined goals (i.e., providing 'operationally defined' targets) 2. Using prompting and prompt fading procedures 3. Frequent feedback from teachers 4. Specification of error correction techniques 5. Task analysis (i.e., breaking down complex skills into smaller steps for teaching) 6. Data collection to monitor progress 7. Generalization These components will be described in more detail in Chapters 3–8.
In vivo ('in life') instruction	Teaching that takes place during real-life situations, such as using functional measurement skills during cooking.
Providing multiple opportunities to practice	Teaching that provides a student with daily repeated opportunities to practice. This can help build students' fluency (accuracy and speed) with basic tool skills (e.g., simple mathematical facts). This in turn means that students can then apply these skills more easily as components of more complex tasks and problem solving, such as using simple addition when purchasing items in shops. Repeated practice can lead to increased competence and confidence with using mathematical knowledge.

A limitation of existing mathematics teaching research with children with developmental disabilities is that most studies have focused only on how best to teach a specific skill, such as how best to teach numeral recognition, or how best to teach single-digit addition. There are very few studies that have described and evaluated structured and comprehensive curricula appropriate for students with a developmental disability that would help educators teach across a number of different numeracy domains. It is also clear from an evaluation of the research that there are very few studies that have described and evaluated a comprehensive sequential curriculum that builds a progression of mathematical skills. Such a sequence might be derived from recommendations for teaching mathematics to neurotypical children in general education. Mathematics Recovery is one such approach that has been used as a comprehensive program to teach mathematics to neurotypical children and has some utility for teaching children with a developmental disability. Although described already in previous books in this series, the Mathematics Recovery approach will be described in more detail in Chapter 2, along with a rationale as to why it might provide a useful starting framework for teaching mathematics to children with a developmental disability. In Chapter 3, we will describe how we have adapted the original Mathematics Recovery approach to suit the learning needs of children with a developmental disability.

Using the book

The assessment materials and lesson plans designed for *Teaching Early Numeracy to Children with Developmental Disabilities* can be downloaded from the website accompanying this book. They can be used for students, like Sheila, in their first years of school (as an 'early' numeracy intervention) or for older children with a developmental disability, like David, who have been in school for some years but who have been struggling with learning numerical skills with regular teaching methods (i.e., it can be used as a 'catch up' intervention). The assessment tools described in Chapter 8 are detailed but can easily support individualized assessment to find out the level of numerical skills children have already acquired (what they already know, or can already do). The lesson plans can be used as a guide for teachers to know exactly 'what to teach next' during individualized instruction. Although teachers can skim the detail and go directly to the lesson plans, the richer detail of the rationale for the teaching methodologies described in the lesson plans is also provided in this book (in Chapters 4–7).

The assessment and teaching materials are described fully in this book and on the accompanying website, however earlier books in the Mathematics Recovery series provide further compatible information on assessment and instruction that will be of interest to the reader. These books are described below. We are convinced that the methods described in this book will contribute enormously to teachers' pedagogical knowledge and time spent teaching children, and so, in turn, lead to much improved learning of numeracy for children with a developmental disability. We believe that children with a developmental disability, including those with autism, can indeed learn what is taught, provided that they are taught systematically using an evidence-based approach. This book describes one such approach.

Who is the book for?

This book will be of benefit to anyone who has an interest in teaching numeracy to children with a developmental disability. Many children with a developmental disability go to mainstream schools, but often general education teachers and paraprofessionals (including teaching assistants) have not received the necessary training or have the relevant experience to know how best to meet these children's learning needs when it comes to teaching mathematics. Thus, the book may be of interest to class teachers, peripatetic teachers and paraprofessionals who support children with a developmental disability who go to a mainstream school.

The teaching materials described in this book could be used as the sole numeracy teaching curriculum, whereby all numeracy teaching is guided by this approach, or to provide supplementary teaching ideas for the typical numeracy instruction provided by a school. For children who go to special education schools, the teaching materials can be used in a similar way, for teachers and teaching assistants to use as the sole teaching approach to numeracy or as an additional teaching resource to the typical numeracy instruction that takes place in school.

Parents too, who may be interested in helping their child acquire more numeracy skills, may also find the book helpful as a guide to teaching in the home. It may be that parents would like to use the book to help identify interesting activities, particularly for them to be able to complement the teaching of specific numeracy skills that they know are being taught in school. At the very least, it is strongly recommended that if schools are using this book with a child, they notify parents to see if they would be interested in working on some of the generalization (extra teaching) activities, described in the lesson plans and in Chapter 7, in the home.

Using the earlier books in the series

This book is the seventh entry in the Mathematics Recovery series. The previous books address instruction and intervention in early number and whole number arithmetic for children from kindergarten to fifth or sixth grade. To distinguish between them, they are often referred to according to the color on the front cover: the blue book, the green book, the red book, the purple book, the orange book and the white book. Brief overviews of these books can be found in the Series Preface earlier in this book.

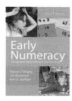    

2

Mathematics Recovery

In Chapter 1 we described how students with developmental disabilities are typically at a considerable educational disadvantage when it comes to learning mathematics in school, compared to their neurotypical peers. Possible explanations for students underperforming in mathematics include that:

- there may be reduced opportunities to learn mathematics
- the structured teaching of mathematics may be underemphasized
- teachers may not be confident that they know the best way to teach mathematics
- teachers may find it difficult to teach mathematic skills, and
- teachers may find it difficult to translate research into practice.

Although the situation appears to be challenging for these children, there is much that we can learn from the research literature regarding how we can improve their learning in mathematics. For example, systematic reviews that have focused on identifying effective mathematical interventions for students with a developmental disability, have repeatedly demonstrated that Systematic Instruction, derived from Applied Behavior Analysis (ABA), can be used with these students and contribute to positive learning outcomes (e.g., Browder et al., 2008). Systematic Instruction, and how it has been applied to the teaching program outlined in this book, will be described in more detail in this chapter and in Chapter 3.

Despite the dominance of Systematic Instruction in the research literature, there are some limitations to the breadth and depth of existing mathematics teaching research with students with developmental disabilities. Very few studies have described and evaluated structured and comprehensive curricula appropriate for students with a developmental disability that would help practitioners teach all numeracy domains. Similarly, there are very few studies that have described and evaluated a comprehensive sequential curriculum that builds a progression of mathematics skills from perceptual counting and numeral identification to more advanced skills such as addition and subtraction in the range 1 to 20 without counting by ones. If teachers were referring to research literature for guidance regarding what and how to teach, as it is recommended that they do, they would be disappointed. There is very little information available to help guide their teaching beyond recommendations for teaching individual skills, such as how best to teach children to select a named numeral from a set of numerals (i.e., numeral recognition) or how best to teach single-digit addition.

One possible solution might be to look outside of the research intended for students with a developmental disability and find out if there are any evidence-based approaches for teaching a full range of mathematical skills that have been evaluated with neurotypical students in general education. It may then be possible to adapt such a program to use with students with a developmental disability. Mathematics Recovery is one such approach that has been used as a comprehensive program to teach numeracy to neurotypical children. Mathematics Recovery has an extensive evidence base demonstrating its applicability and positive learning outcomes for neurotypical students in mainstream schools.

In the first and second sections of this chapter, we will describe the Mathematics Recovery approach in some detail, including the theoretical framework for the approach as well as the key guiding principles and characteristics of instruction. In the final section in this chapter, we will explain why we believe that Mathematics Recovery provides a useful framework for teaching numeracy to students with a developmental disability. In Chapter 3, we will describe how the original Mathematics Recovery has been adapted in this book to suit the learning needs of students with a developmental disability.

Background to Mathematics Recovery

Mathematics Recovery was developed in Australia in the 1990s (Wright et al., 1994, 2006b), and was intended as a tool for intensive, individualized numeracy teaching for 'at-risk' students in mainstream classrooms who demonstrated low attainment after their first year in school (i.e., when they were 6–7 years old). The aim of the teaching was to advance the child to an average level for their class (hence the term, Mathematics Recovery).

Mathematics Recovery instructional frameworks

The Mathematics Recovery early numeracy program is based on an instructional framework. This framework was first described in *Teaching Number*, 'the green book', where five progressive stages in children's development of early arithmetic strategies are identified.

Descriptions of the typical skills that a child demonstrates at each of the developmental stages are summarized in Table 2.1.

Table 2.1 Five progressive stages in children's development of early arithmetic strategies

Developmental stage	Typical skills of a student at this stage
Emergent	The child might have some knowledge of number words and numerals but does not have perceptual counting strategies. That is, they either do not know the number words or cannot coordinate the number words with items.
Perceptual	The child can count items when they can see, hear or feel the items.
Figurative	The child can count well and use 'counting-all' strategies to add. That is, they are able to count to find out the total number of objects in two screened collections. They can also do some simple subtraction tasks involving screened collections.
Counting on	The student can use counting on and counting back to solve simple addition and subtraction tasks in the range 1 to 20, involving screened collections. They might be able to read numerals up to 100 but typically have little understanding of place value.
Facile	The student knows some number facts in the range 1 to 20 and has developed a wide range of strategies other than counting by ones to solve addition and subtraction tasks in the range 1 to 20, presented as bare number tasks. As well, they might have multiplicative strategies based on repeated addition.

For each developmental stage, the green book also provides descriptions of six key topics, each of which is considered to be an important focus of teaching for a child at each of the progressive stages. The key topics fall into one of the following three categories: (a) Number Words and Numerals, (b) Counting, and (c) Grouping. Table 2.2 sets out the corresponding key topics for each of the developmental stages. Also indicated in Table 2.2 for each key topic is: (1) its category (W – Number Words and Numerals, C – Counting or G – Grouping), (2) its teaching focus, and (3) the number of teaching activities within the key topic. The teaching activities are progressively more difficult, such that students would not be expected to work on the later teaching activities within each key topic until such time that they have demonstrated mastery with the earlier teaching activities. In total, there are 182 recommended teaching procedures across the five developmental stages of mathematical competence.

Table 2.2   The titles and foci of the key topics across the developmental stages

Category	Developmental stage and key topic title	Focus of key topic	No. of teaching procedures
	Emergent		
W	Number Word Sequences from 1 to 20	Knowledge of forward number word sequences in the range 1 to 20 and backward number word sequences in the range 1 to 10	7
W	Numerals from 1 to 10	Knowledge of numerals and numeral sequences in the range 1 to 10	6
C	Counting Visible Items	Perceptual counting strategies	5
G	Spatial Patterns	Initial facility to ascribe number to spatial patterns and random arrays	3
G	Finger Patterns	Initial facility with making finger patterns	7
C	Temporal Patterns and Temporal Sequences	Facility with copying and counting temporal patterns and temporal sequences	4 = 32
	Perceptual		
W	Number Word Sequences from 1 to 30	Knowledge of forward and backward number word sequences in the range 1 to 30	7
W	Numerals from 1 to 20	Knowledge of numerals and numeral sequences in the range 1 to 20	6
C	Figurative Counting	Figurative counting strategies	4
G	Spatial Patterns	Facility to ascribe number to regular spatial patterns	5
G	Finger Patterns	Facility with making finger patterns for numbers in the range 1 to 10	4
G	Equal Groups and Sharing	Initial ideas of equal groups and equal sharing	6 = 32
	Figurative		
W	Number Word Sequences from 1 to 100	Knowledge of forward and backward number word sequences in the range 1 to 100	7

Category	Developmental stage and key topic title	Focus of key topic	No. of teaching procedures
W	Numerals from 1 to 100	Knowledge of numerals in the range 1 to 100	10
C	Counting on and Counting back	Counting strategies involving counting on and counting back	7
G	Combining and Partitioning Involving 5 and 10	Facility with using 5 and 10 to combine and partition numbers in the range 1 to 10	6
G	Partitioning and Combining Numbers in the Range 1 to 10	Facility with partitioning and combining numbers in the range 1 to 10	7
G	Early Multiplication and Division	Early multiplicative and divisional strategies	6 = **43**
	Counting on		
W	Number Word Sequences by 2s, 10s, 5s, 3s and 4s	Facility with forward and backward number word sequences by 2s, 10s, 5s, 3s and 4s in the range 1 to 100	8
W	Numerals from 1 to 1,000	Knowledge of numerals in the range 1 to 1,000	7
C	Incrementing by 10s and 1s	The facility to increment and decrement numbers by 10s and 1s, in the range 1 to 100	4
G	Adding and Subtracting to and from Decade Numbers	The facility to add and subtract in the range 1 to 10, and to add and subtract involving a decade number and a number in the range 1 to 10	6
G	Addition and Subtraction to 20, using 5 and 10	Facility with addition and subtraction in the range 1 to 20, using grouping by 5 and 10	9
G	Developing Multiplication and Division	Early multiplicative and divisional strategies	7 = **41**
	Facile		
W	Counting by 10s and 100s	Facility with counting forward and backward by 10s on and off the decade and counting by 100s on and off the 100, and on and off the decade	6

(Continued)

Table 2.2   (Continued)

Category	Developmental stage and key topic title	Focus of key topic	No. of teaching procedures
C	2-digit Addition and Subtraction through Counting	Counting-based strategies for 2-digit addition and subtraction	7
G	Non-canonical Forms of 2-digit and 3-digit Numbers	Facility to associate non-canonical forms of 2-digit and 3-digit numbers with their canonical forms	5
G	2-digit Addition and Subtraction through Collections	Collections-based strategies for 2-digit addition and subtraction	6
G	Higher Decade Addition and Subtraction	Strategies for adding numbers in the range 2 to 9 to 2-digit numbers, and subtracting numbers in the range 2 to 9, from 2-digit numbers	4
G	Advanced Multiplication and Division	Advanced multiplicative and divisional strategies	6 = 34
			182

The instructional framework outlined in the green book (Table 4.2, pp. 69–70) underpins the *Teaching Early Numeracy to Children with Developmental Disabilities* program in this book, which is well structured and systematic: numeracy targets are organized both horizontally (different groups of activities within the same ability level – key topics) and vertically (progressive stages of difficulty).

More recently, the Mathematics Recovery framework has been revised and extended and is described in the white book. The revised framework is referred to as *The Learning Framework in Number* and its focus is the arithmetic typically taught in the first five years of school. The Learning Framework in Number spans three broad bands of number learning: Very Early Number, Early Number and Middle Number. Table 2.3 sets out the three bands and indicative age ranges for each. Across the three bands, the Learning Framework in Number identifies nine domains of number learning. The domains range from very early knowledge of number words and numerals to multiplication and division in the range 1 to 100 and beyond. The arithmetic knowledge just described could also be referred to as whole number arithmetic.

Table 2.3 Bands and domains in the Learning Framework in Number (LFIN)

Broad bands	Ages	Domains	
1. Very Early Number (VEN)	2 to 5	1.	Very Early Number
2. Early Number (EN)	4 to 8	2A.	Early Number Words & Numerals
		2B.	Early Structuring
		2C.	Early Arithmetical Strategies
3. Middle Number (MN)	6 to 10	3A.	Number Words & Numerals
		3B.	Structuring Numbers 1 to 20
		3C.	Conceptual Place Value
		3D.	Addition and Subtraction to 100
		3E.	Early Multiplication & Division
		3F.	Multiplicative Basic Facts

Overview of Band 2

This overview will focus on Band 2, the three domains of early number knowledge: 2A. Early Number Words and Numerals, 2B. Early Structuring, and 2C. Early Arithmetical Strategies. This band most closely represents the framework for the Emergent, Perceptual and Figurative key topics from the green book, on which *Teaching Early Numeracy to Children with Developmental Disabilities* is based.

2A. Early Number Words and Numerals

This domain involves knowledge of basic spoken number word sequences by ones, both forward and backward, such as 'one, two, three...twenty' and 'thirty-two, thirty-one, thirty, twenty-nine, twenty-eight'. This Learning Framework in Number domain also involves reading and writing numerals (although writing numerals was not included in the green book and thus is not a part of *Teaching Early Numeracy to Children with Developmental Disabilities*). For both number words and numerals, the domain focuses on the range up to 100. This domain focuses on children's emerging knowledge of number words and numerals.

2B. Early Structuring

This domain involves knowledge of finger patterns for numbers up to 10, and standard spatial configurations such as dice and domino patterns. The domain also involves knowledge of small combinations and partitions, such as small doubles (1&1, 2&2,

3&3, 4&4, 5&5) and five pluses (5&1, 5&2, 5&3, 5&4, 5&5), and additional emerging knowledge of addition and subtraction in the range 1 to 10.

2C. Early Arithmetical Strategies

Early arithmetical strategies refers to a progression of counting-based strategies that students use to solve counting, additive and subtractive tasks, such as counting the items in a collection, determining the number of items in two collections or the number of items remaining after some items are removed. These strategies arise in situations where the items to be counted are in the child's visual field or are screened and thus unavailable to count perceptually. These strategies include the advanced counting-by-ones strategies, that is, counting on and counting back.

The curriculum for teaching early numeracy to students with developmental disabilities described in this book has been developed from the earlier frameworks and tools described in the green book. However, some teachers may be more familiar with the Learning Framework in Number from the more recently published white book. The two frameworks, however, are not mutually exclusive, and both provide detailed information related to many aspects of the *Teaching Early Numeracy for Children with Developmental Disabilities* program, and to our general approach to instruction. Table 2.4 sets out, for the Early Number domain in the Learning Framework in Number, the key topics from the green book. This is so that the reader can clearly see the interconnectedness and relatedness of the two frameworks. Band 2 only includes recommended teaching procedures from the Emergent, Perceptual and Figurative developmental phases. *Teaching Early Numeracy to Children with Developmental Disabilities* does not include any teaching procedures from the Very Early Number or the Middle Number domains. Thus, early multiplication and division teaching activities from the perceptual and figurative key topics that fall under Band 3, The Middle Number domain, are not included in the lesson plans accompanying this book.

Table 2.4   Links to the green book key topics

Learning Framework in Number: Early Number domains	Developmental phase and corresponding 'green book' key topics
2A. Early Number Words & Numerals	Emergent Number Word Sequences from 1 to 20 Numerals from 1 to 10 Perceptual Number Word Sequences from 1 to 30 Numerals from 1 to 20 Figurative Number Word Sequences from 1 to 100 Numerals from 1 to 100

Learning Framework in Number: Early Number domains	Developmental phase and corresponding 'green book' key topics
2B. Early Structuring	Emergent
	Spatial Patterns
	Finger Patterns
	Perceptual
	Spatial Patterns
	Finger Patterns
	Figurative
	Combining and Partitioning Involving Five and Ten
	Partitioning and Combining Numbers in the Range 1 to 10
2C. Early Arithmetical Strategies	Emergent
	Counting Visible Items
	Temporal Patterns and Temporal Sequences
	Perceptual
	Figurative Counting
	Figurative
	Counting on and Counting back

Theoretical basis for Mathematics Recovery

The theoretical basis for Mathematics Recovery draws in a very significant way on the early number research program undertaken in the 1980s at the University of Georgia (e.g., Steffe & Cobb, 1988). Underlying the work of Steffe and colleagues is von Glasersfeld's (1984, 1991) radical constructivist view, that draws extensively on Piaget's theory of cognitive development. This includes, but is not limited to, a theory about how students construct mathematical strategies. According to von Glasersfeld (1991), a key idea in constructivist ideology is the notion that originated with Socrates, viz that 'knowledge is the result of a learner's activity rather than of the passive reception of information or instruction' (von Glasersfeld, 1991, p. xiv).

To find out more about how students come to construct their mathematical knowledge, around the mid-1970s Steffe developed and used a research methodology called 'constructivist teaching experiments' (Steffe, 1991). This methodology involved detailed observation and study of students learning in the context of their intensive teaching sessions. The goal of this research was to develop psychological models to explain and predict students' mathematical learning and development. Embedded in this approach is the identification of the strategies that the student uses in situations that are problematic for them, and how these strategies develop and are reorganized over the course of an extended teaching cycle, as observed in teaching sessions mainly, but also in pre- and post-interview-based assessments.

Key aspects of Steffe's constructivist teaching experiment methodology *per se* have been adapted as a basis for the Mathematics Recovery program, including an emphasis on routinely videotaping assessment and teaching sessions. These are used extensively in the evaluation of instructional activities and for the professional development of teachers. Other similarities include, but are not limited to, Steffe's students being of similar age and achievement levels to those who use Mathematics Recovery, there being a focus on intensive individualized teaching, and teaching sessions occurring several times per week in cycles of 18–20 weeks during the student's second year of school. Accordingly, the intervention procedure for neurotypical students who use Mathematics Recovery usually involves the following steps:

1. A trained teacher conducts an individualized assessment interview with the student. The interview has two purposes: (1) to determine their current numeracy stage – this is referred to as the *profile* of the student's knowledge; and (2) to document the student's strategies, errors and difficulties, as revealed in the interview – this is referred to as the *portrait* of the student's knowledge. The assessment is video recorded to enable determining the student's stage and documenting their strategies at a later time.

2. Based on the assessment results, the interviewer determines the student's current stage and levels on three models of student progressions: 2A, 2B and 2C. Activities from different key topics that will help advance the student's strategies are then selected.

3. The student is taught intensively on an individual basis for 30 minutes a day, four to five times a week, for approximately 12–15 weeks.

4. At the end of the intervention period, the assessment interview is repeated. If the student has made satisfactory progress, they resume group mathematics instruction with the rest of their class.

A fundamental question in Steffe's research and for Mathematics Recovery, is 'What kind of instruction supports students' construction of arithmetic knowledge?' The section below exemplifies how constructivism underpins the Mathematics Recovery approach to instruction. Some comparisons are also provided regarding the similarities and differences between the constructivist approach underpinning teaching in Mathematics Recovery and Systematic Instruction.

Instruction: principles and characteristics

The description of the approach for individualized teaching in Mathematics Recovery is organized into three sections: (1) Guiding principles; (2) Characteristics of children's problem solving, and (3) Key elements of instruction, all of which require teachers to be able to embed both theoretical and practical learning into their teaching. These are described in more detail in Chapter 2 of the green book and in Chapter 5 of the white book, but are summarized briefly below.

Guiding principles of instruction

There are nine guiding principles of instruction that provide the basis for the day-to-day enquiry-based Mathematics Recovery instruction. These are described on page 93 of the white book and are summarized below:

1. *Enquiry-based/problem-based teaching.* The teaching approach is enquiry based, that is problem based. Students routinely are engaged in thinking hard to solve numerical problems which, for them, are quite challenging.
2. *Initial and ongoing assessment.* Teaching is informed by an initial comprehensive assessment and ongoing assessment through teaching. The latter refers to the teacher's informed understanding of the child's current knowledge and problem-solving strategies, and continual revision of this understanding.
3. *Teaching just beyond the cutting edge.* Teaching is focused just beyond the cutting edge of the child's current knowledge.
4. *Selecting from a bank of teaching procedures.* Teachers exercise their professional judgment in selecting from a bank of teaching procedures, each of which involves particular instructional settings and tasks, and varying this selection on the basis of ongoing observations.
5. *Engendering more sophisticated strategies.* The teacher understands children's numerical strategies and deliberately engenders the development of more sophisticated strategies.
6. *Observing the child and fine-tuning teaching.* Teaching involves intensive, ongoing observation by the teacher and continual micro-adjusting or fine-tuning of teaching on the basis of his or her observation of student responses.
7. *Incorporating symbolizing and notating.* Teaching supports and builds on the child's intuitive, verbally-based strategies and these are used as a basis for the development of written forms of arithmetic which accord with the child's verbally-based strategies.
8. *Encouraging sustained thinking and reflection.* The teacher provides the child with sufficient time to solve a given problem. Consequently, the child is frequently engaged in episodes which involve sustained thinking, reflection on his or her thinking and reflecting on the results of his or her thinking. Silent thinking is the norm during teaching sessions.
9. *Aiming for children's intrinsic satisfaction.* Students gain intrinsic satisfaction from their problem solving, from their realization that they are making progress, and from the verification methods they develop.

Mathematics Recovery has many guiding principles of instruction that are consistent with those recommended for Systematic Instruction. This highlights the compatibility of the two approaches. For example, although the methodology may differ, both approaches have an emphasis on pre-assessment and ongoing assessment throughout teaching (see Chapter 8 for a description of pre-assessment and for an overview of ongoing data collection and assessment). Chapters 4–7 also illustrate how in Systematic

Instruction teachers can use their professional judgment in selecting from a bank of teaching procedures or in how to make small moment-by-moment adjustments in their teaching which are informed by their observation of student responses. In Systematic Instruction, there is less of a focus on aiming for intrinsic satisfaction through problem solving. However, there is recognition that students may require more extrinsic motivators during teaching (see Chapter 4).

Characteristics of children's problem solving

There are also nine characteristics of children's problem solving and learning that provide the framework for Mathematics Recovery individualized instruction. Teachers learn to judge a student's response in terms of these characteristics and modify their teaching accordingly. These are described on p. 93 of the white book and are summarized below:

1. *Cognitive reorganization* refers to a qualitative change in the way the child regards the problem and generation of a strategy that was previously unavailable to the child.
2. *Anticipation* refers to a realization by the child prior to using a strategy that the strategy will lead to a particular result.
3. *Curtailment* refers to the mental process of cutting short an aspect of a problem-solving activity when, prior to commencing the activity, the child has an awareness of the results of the activity and thus the activity becomes redundant.
4. *Re-presentation* refers to a kind of cognitive activity akin to a mental replay, during which the child presents again to herself or himself, a prior cognitive experience.
5. *Spontaneity, robustness and certitude.* A child's strategy is spontaneous when it arises without assistance. A child's strategy is robust when the child is able to use the same strategy over a wide range of similar problems. Certitude refers to a child's assuredness and confidence about the correctness of their solution to a problem.
6. *Asserting autonomy.* Students sometimes assert their autonomy as problem solvers, by imploring the teacher not to help them or to allow them sufficient time to solve a problem independently.
7. *Child engagement.* The ideal situation in the teaching sessions is for the child to apply himself or herself directly and with effort when presented with a problem, and to remain engaged in solving the problem for a relatively extended period if necessary.
8. *Child reflection* refers specifically to a child reflecting on their own prior thinking or the results of their thinking, which can lead to the child becoming explicitly aware of elements of their thinking that were not consciously part of their thinking prior to the period of reflection.
9. *Enjoying the challenge of problem solving.* There are many instances in the individualized teaching sessions where students seem to revel in challenging problem solving, and ultimately they can come to regard problem solving as an intrinsically satisfying and rewarding experience.

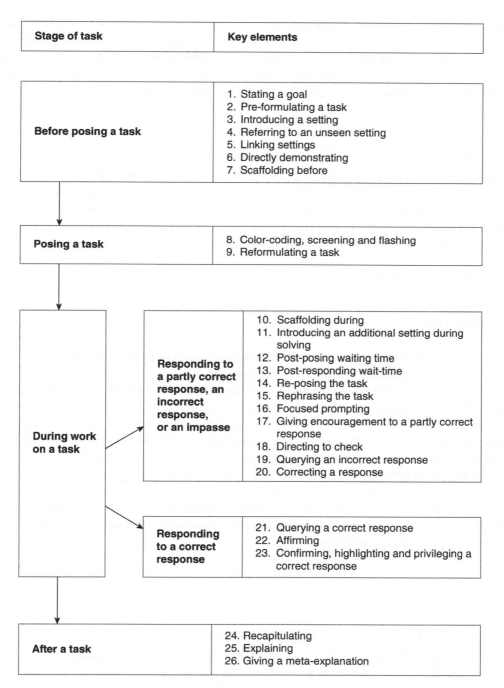

Stage of task	Key elements
Before posing a task	1. Stating a goal 2. Pre-formulating a task 3. Introducing a setting 4. Referring to an unseen setting 5. Linking settings 6. Directly demonstrating 7. Scaffolding before
Posing a task	8. Color-coding, screening and flashing 9. Reformulating a task
During work on a task — **Responding to a partly correct response, an incorrect response, or an impasse**	10. Scaffolding during 11. Introducing an additional setting during solving 12. Post-posing waiting time 13. Post-responding wait-time 14. Re-posing the task 15. Rephrasing the task 16. Focused prompting 17. Giving encouragement to a partly correct response 18. Directing to check 19. Querying an incorrect response 20. Correcting a response
During work on a task — **Responding to a correct response**	21. Querying a correct response 22. Affirming 23. Confirming, highlighting and privileging a correct response
After a task	24. Recapitulating 25. Explaining 26. Giving a meta-explanation

Figure 2.1 A framework of 26 key elements of teaching in Mathematics Recovery

Again, there are some similarities between the ideas presented here and those which are embedded in a Systematic Instruction approach. For example, the characteristics of spontaneity, robustness and certitude are conceptually similar to that of 'fluency' in Systematic Instruction: that is, that for a skill to be learnt, students should be able to respond not only consistently and accurately but quickly as well (i.e., fluently; see Binder, 1996).

Key elements of intensive one-to-one instruction

The key elements of one-to-one instruction are micro-instructional strategies used by a teacher when interacting with a student in posing and solving an arithmetical task. The key elements chart in Figure 2.1 presents a framework of 26 key elements, developed from the work of Wright et al. (2006b) and Tran (2016). The framework is organized into four stages of a teacher's working through a task:

- Before posing a task
- Posing a task
- During work on a task
- After a task

Chapter 5 of the white book describes and illustrates each of these principles and characteristics in detail and they are only summarized here.

Included among the key elements of teaching in Mathematics Recovery is the process of scaffolding. Scaffolding refers to the help that the teacher provides when the child is struggling, in the form of access to materials or teacher modeling. Also recommended is a general approach to introducing a novel instructional setting and the use of instructional techniques such as flashing (briefly displaying) and screening (hiding from view), as well as careful use of color coding. These elements are all functionally similar to the prompting and prompt fading techniques used in Systematic Instruction (described in Chapter 6). The key instructional elements for responding to a partly correct response, an incorrect response, or an impasse also have some aspects in common with the recommended error correction procedures (see Chapter 6).

Integration of constructivist and Systematic Instruction teaching approaches

We have described the approach for individualized teaching in Mathematics Recovery and given examples of similarities between the Mathematics Recovery approach underpinned by constructivism and Systematic Instruction. It is important to consider too that teaching approaches developed for students in general education may not always be completely accessible for students with a developmental disability who do not have the high level of critical or abstract thinking skills, such as problem solving and analysis, required for this approach (Browder & Spooner, 2011; Rizzo & Taylor, 2016).

The debate about what sort of teaching approaches different students may need rests predominantly on how students learn and the extent to which different students may require structures and supports from their teachers to be able to learn new skills and knowledge. Instructional approaches can be put on a continuum of how much guidance is needed to teach new skills. Thus, Systematic Instruction can be thought of as providing more support for children's learning than more constructivist approaches, at least in the early stages of teaching.

Table 2.5 illustrates this view by highlighting some of the key similarities and differences between the Mathematics Recovery approach underpinned by constructivism and Systematic Instruction (adapted from Przychodzin et al., 2004).

Table 2.5 Key similarities and differences between the constructivist approach to teaching mathematics and Systematic Instruction

Constructivist approach	Systematic Instruction
Emphasis on improving the learning/teaching process	
Considers previous knowledge with regard to what should be taught next	
Teacher facilitates enquiry or discovery-based problem solving	Teacher directly teaches new concepts or rules
Students construct their own learning based on their current understanding of the world and their own personal discovery and experimentation	Comprehensive set of instructions provided for organizing delivery of teaching to guide students' acquisition, retention and generalization of new knowledge
Four components of effective instruction (e.g., Steele, 2005):	Three components of effective instruction (e.g., Stein et al., 2006):
1. Lessons are related to real-life situations to make the ideas more meaningful 2. Lessons begin with information and examples that are familiar to the students (from their own experiences) 3. Teaching activities are designed so that students are actively involved in the lesson 4. Teachers integrate high-level thinking skills, and provide clear explanations and guidance to clarify ideas	1. Effective instructional design, with an emphasis on providing clearly defined teaching objectives 2. Effective instructional delivery, with an emphasis on repetitive practice and error correction procedures 3. Organization and effective use of resources, particularly time
Lessons should be inherently motivating	External motivators may be needed to facilitate students' acquisition of new skills

One of the key differences between the two approaches is the contrast between enquiry-based/problem-based teaching in constructivism and the more direct skills teaching in Systematic Instruction. Constructivist teachers encourage students to be active learners who construct their own knowledge rather than having it directly delivered or transmitted to them. Students may be given an ill-defined question or problem or be encouraged to generate their own questions. In solving the problem or answering the question, students gain knowledge. The teacher's role is characterized by minimal teacher guidance and structure as students use their own experiences to discover or construct essential information for themselves. Systematic Instruction, on the other hand, is more centered on transmission of knowledge from the teacher to the student, rather than on construction of knowledge by the student. Teachers may more actively structure content and present very specific content to the student. Systematic Instruction teachers usually use a comprehensive set of guidelines for organizing their teaching, including a focus on three components of effective design believed to be absolutely central to students' acquisition of new skills: (a) instructional design, (b) instructional delivery, with an emphasis on repetitive practice and error correction procedures, and (c) organization and effective use of resources (e.g., Stein et al., 2006).

These components will be described in more detail in the next chapter and elsewhere in the book. By providing a more structured and guided approach in the form of Systematic Instruction, students with a developmental disability can focus in on what exactly it is that needs to be learnt and how to learn it, rather than trying to take in and manipulate complex and novel information, and connect it with their prior knowledge to work out how to solve a problem for themselves.

Although both approaches encourage social interaction between a student and a teacher, social interaction in constructivist lessons encourages students to be able to verbalize their thinking with teachers, to brainstorm possible problem-solving strategies and to share the ideas they are constructing. They often reach a solution through trial and error and explain to their teachers how they came up with their answers. For students with developmental disabilities who may have significant language delay, this can be difficult. In Systematic Instruction, students learn new skills as they respond to questions or comments from the teacher based upon their prior experience of their social interactions with others and the results of their actions. A behavior that results in a positive consequence from their teacher is more likely to be repeated, while a behavior that results in a neutral or more negative reaction is less likely to occur. It is through this process that learning occurs (see Chapter 4).

There is also less focus on aiming for intrinsic satisfaction through problem solving in Systematic Instruction. Rather, lessons do not need to be inherently motivating if students' learning and motivation can be encouraged through the use of external motivators (see Chapter 4).

Why Mathematics Recovery might provide a useful framework for students with developmental disabilities

Although there are some conceptual differences between the Mathematics Recovery approach underpinned by constructivism and Systematic Instruction, there are nevertheless several reasons why Mathematics Recovery may provide a useful framework to adapt for teaching mathematics to students with a developmental disability. These are summarized in Table 2.6.

Table 2.6 Rationale for using Mathematics Recovery as a framework for teaching students with a developmental disability

1.	It is an evidence-based teaching approach
2.	It offers a comprehensive approach to arithmetic content
3.	It can be used with students who have yet to acquire any numeracy knowledge or skills
4.	It involves an individualized teaching approach
5.	It has many elements consistent with Systematic Instruction

It is an evidence-based teaching approach

In Chapter 1 we described how important it is for teachers to apply educational practices that have been shown to have research support and that they should use 'evidence-based practices' to impart skills to students (No Child Left Behind [NCLB], 2002). Although systematic reviews have highlighted that Systematic Instruction should be the method of choice for teaching mathematics learning for students with a developmental disability, most of the studies described in the reviews focus only on teaching isolated mathematical skills rather than a comprehensive skill set. Thus, it is important that educators of students with developmental disabilities look to see if there are any evidence-based approaches for teaching a full range of mathematical skills that have been evaluated with neurotypical students in general education. Mathematics Recovery is one such approach that has an impressive evidence base.

The early development of Mathematics Recovery was informed by extensive research on how students construct their numerical knowledge (i.e., through the constructivist teaching experiment methodology conducted by Steffe and colleagues in the 1980s). In addition, existing data on the program's use with neurotypical students show it to be effective. Mathematics Recovery has been successfully implemented in several countries, including Australia, New Zealand, the UK, Canada and the USA (e.g., Smith et al., 2010;

Willey et al., 2007; Wright, 2003; Wright et al., 1994). For example, in UK research, 210 low-attaining students received individualized teaching for 20 half-hour sessions, three or four times a week (Willey et al., 2007). Pre- and post-test data based on the Mathematics Recovery assessment tools showed that after intervention 48% of the participants had gained two arithmetic stages, 27% one stage, 15% three stages, and although 6% had remained at the same stage they had nevertheless still improved their numeracy skills.

In addition to its use as an individualized intervention tool, Mathematics Recovery has been used as a model for whole classroom teaching with typical learners. The 'Count Me in Too' numeracy program, which has been successfully implemented in more than 1,000 Australian and New Zealand primary schools (Bobis et al., 2005; Thomas & Ward, 2001), is an adaptation of Mathematics Recovery, also developed by Wright (2003). Practitioners in other countries, including the USA and the UK, have also adopted the whole classroom teaching model.

We know how crucial it is to use evidence-based practices when teaching students with a developmental disability, so the existing evidence base for Mathematics Recovery makes it particularly appealing to use as a framework for developing an approach for teaching mathematics to such students (see Tabor, 2018 for a comprehensive summary of the research underpinning Mathematics Recovery).

It offers a comprehensive approach to arithmetic content

One appealing feature of the Mathematics Recovery approach is that it provides a comprehensive sequential program that builds a detailed progression of numerical skills from basic to more advanced. As mentioned previously, there are few comprehensive curricula available for teaching mathematics to students with a developmental disability, so it is important to consider adapting approaches that have already been developed to use with neurotypical students in general education.

It can be used with students who have yet to acquire any numeracy knowledge or skills

Mathematics Recovery was developed for low-attaining students in their first years of school who were struggling with even quite basic number processes such as counting with one-to-one correspondence and numeral recognition. As such, the program is suitable for students with a developmental disability who have not yet received any mathematics teaching (i.e., it can be used as a 'first' numeracy intervention). It can, however, also be used with older students with a developmental disability who have already had some regular classroom mathematics but who struggled to gain basic knowledge and skills during their earlier education (i.e., it can also be used as a 'catch up' numeracy program, even for older students who have no or very little knowledge of and skills in early number domains).

It involves an individualized teaching approach

Mathematics Recovery was developed initially to be used as an individualized teaching approach for neurotypical students who had been identified as struggling in mathematics. For students with a developmental disability, this individualized approach is also extremely important as it means that teaching can be adapted to meet each child's particular needs. This is particularly crucial considering the wide variation of ability levels within the general developmental disability population.

It has many elements consistent with Systematic Instruction

Finally, there are common elements in the Mathematics Recovery program that would facilitate compatibility with the evidence-based Systematic Instruction teaching methods. For example, teaching strategies like 'micro-adjusting' and 'scaffolding' that were described previously are functionally similar to prompting and prompt fading which are common practices in Systematic Instruction.

In addition, most individual teaching activities described in Mathematics Recovery are divided into small, progressive steps in much the same way as a task analysis is used in Systematic Instruction to break complex skills into easier, more teachable units. Another key idea associated with constructivist theory is that learning should be meaningful and related to real-life situations (Grobecker, 1999), and this has parallels with the idea of 'generalization' integral to any Systematic Instruction approach to teaching (see Chapter 7).

Despite the obvious advantages of using the Mathematics Recovery program to teach numeracy to students with a developmental disability, it should be apparent that not all of the teaching approaches incorporated into the model will be completely accessible for students with a developmental disability. More specific and structured guidance may be required from teachers for students to learn new mathematical skills, and this may be best achieved through following a Systematic Instruction approach.

There is no need, however, for educators to have to choose between using *only* Systematic Instruction or *only* a constructivist approach. The approaches are not mutually exclusive, and it is possible to combine them. One of the main aims of this book is to describe an approach that has integrated ideas from both perspectives, to maximize results in teaching numeracy to learners with a developmental disability. In Chapter 3 we will describe how the original Mathematics Recovery program has been adapted in this book to suit the learning needs of students with a developmental disability.

3

Adapting Mathematics Recovery

The approach presented in this book is drawn from a program of numeracy research and development projects which have been implemented in several schools in the UK and Norway since early 2000. Many of these implementations have taken place within the *Teaching Early Numeracy to Children with Developmental Disabilities* program. A key part of our development of the program was our research into the impact that deficits associated with developmental disability (including autism) might have on core aspects of children's academic learning and any related issues that might arise in connection with teaching mathematical content. We then started to make some adjustments to the description of the teaching procedures described in the green book to accommodate these difficulties, at the same time as integrating ideas from both constructivist and Systematic Instruction teaching methodologies.

In Chapter 1, Systematic Instruction was described as 'teaching focused on specific, measurable responses that may either be discrete (singular) or a response chain (e.g., task analysis), and that are established through the use of defined methods of prompting and feedback based on the principles and research of Applied Behavior Analysis' (Browder, 2001, p. 95). Systematic Instruction has several important components, including using clearly defined teaching goals (i.e., 'operationally defined' targets), using a system of prompting and prompt fading techniques, specification of error correction techniques, data collection to monitor progress, and generalization (Browder & Spooner, 2011).

A summary of these modifications to Mathematics Recovery is provided in this chapter, but the key principles are elaborated on throughout the book. We will describe the adaptations we made to the original Mathematics Recovery program in the context of:

1. Adapting the lesson plans (i.e., *what* to teach)
2. Adapting the Mathematics Recovery teaching approach (i.e., *how* best to teach)

We conclude this chapter by summarizing the research evidence to date for using the approach set out in this book with children with a developmental disability.

Adapting the lesson plans

In Chapter 2, we described how Systematic Instruction approaches provide a comprehensive set of ideas for organizing teaching for children. This has been achieved by developing detailed lesson plans for several of the Mathematics Recovery teaching procedures summarized in Table 2.2. These lesson plans can be downloaded from the website accompanying this book and they provide teachers with clear, accurate and unambiguous instructions for organizing their delivery of teaching that can maximize students' acquisition, retention and generalization of new mathematical skills.

Sequence of skills and concepts

To develop the lesson plans, we first considered the sequence of skills and concepts to be taught that had been recommended in Mathematics Recovery (see Table 2.2). This is important as the order in which information and skills are introduced affects the difficulty students have in learning them. Sequencing skills and concepts involves determining the optimum order for introducing new information and strategies such that easy skills should always be taught before more difficult ones, and that strategies and information that are likely to be confused are not introduced consecutively.

As described in Chapter 2, the sequence of skills and concepts to be taught in Mathematics Recovery is well structured and systematic: numeracy targets are organized both horizontally (different groups of activities within the same ability level – key topics) and vertically (progressive stages of difficulty). As these instructional sequences are so clear and comprehensive, there was no need to change the sequence of introduction for various skills in this book and our scope and sequence of skills is the same as in the original Mathematics Recovery program.

Nonetheless, we recognized that, for some students, the teaching units would need to be broken down even further into smaller, even more manageable segments for teaching. This process is called a *task analysis*. For example, an activity from the Temporal Patterns and Temporal Sequences key topic in the Emergent Stage (see lesson plan A6.1: Copying and Counting Temporal Sequences of Movements) requires a student to be able to provide the correct number of hand chops when provided with a given number (e.g., 'make four hand chops'). In the lesson plan for teaching this skill, we broke it down into additional teaching steps:

1. The teacher and student do the hand chops simultaneously, with both the teacher and student counting out loud.
2. The teacher does the hand chops while the student counts them (the teacher does not count).
3. The student does the hand chops while the teacher counts them (the student does not need to count, although they can if they want to).
4. The student makes the hand chops and counts.

This detailed breakdown of skills into very small steps, and working on only one component of a skill at a time and gradually building up to putting all components together, is particularly useful for many children with a developmental disability. This is because they can easily become frustrated and overwhelmed if the material or instructions presented to them initially are too complex.

Specification of short, succinct verbal instructions

Children with developmental disabilities may have difficulty with memory and auditory perception, as well as communication impairments that can affect academic performance. This may result in students finding it difficult to process and understand teachers' questions, especially if they are wordy or complicated. In the lesson plans, to accommodate any potential difficulties with language processing, we specify short, succinct verbal instructions for teachers to use for most teaching activities. For example, when teaching identification of numerals, rather than the teacher delivering an instruction using five words, 'point to the number 2', this has been changed to a simple two-word instruction, 'touch 2' (see lesson plan A2.4: Numeral Recognition). Sometimes the wording of the instruction has been changed in the main teaching procedure section of the lesson plan, as with the previous example. On other occasions, however, if it was felt important to convey the essence of the original instruction from the green book, recommendations for changing the wording are provided only in the 'help that may be provided' section of the lesson plan and not in the main teaching procedure section.

Specification of prompting and prompt fading techniques

Another modification in the lesson plans provided is clear specification of recommended *prompting* strategies for each target skill. These appear in the 'help that may be provided' section. We know that the cognitive profiles of children with a developmental disability may vary greatly and that any descriptions of teaching procedures would need to have the scope to be able to be individually modified to meet the needs of children with a wide range of cognitive impairment. For children with more severe developmental disabilities, we describe how to use higher levels of prompting than outlined in the green book, especially for when new skills are presented to students for the very first time and they are not sure how to respond.

In these instances, the teacher would present the task with a prompt, thus partially helping the student to respond. Once the student is able to respond correctly when the prompt is provided, the teacher attempts the removal of the prompt (*prompt fading*) during the following presentations. Prompting suggestions for each target skill are included in the lesson plans. These strategies correspond to different levels of assistance so that the teacher can adapt the teaching procedure to individual students' needs. For numeral recognition where a child is required to select a named numeral from a set of displayed numerals, the recommended prompting strategies include *pointing prompts* (the teacher points to the correct card), *positional prompts* (e.g., placing the correct card closer to the child) and *physical guidance prompts* (e.g., the teacher places the child's hand on the correct card).

For many students with developmental disabilities, including autism, using visual support prompts can greatly enhance learning (Hayes et al., 2010). In the lesson plans, recommendations for using *visual prompts* to help a child master tasks they are struggling with are also provided. For example, if a child is asked to count from 1 to 5 and does not usually stop counting at 5, the teacher is advised to hold up a numeral 5 card as a reminder to stop counting. The teacher would then fade (gradually stop using) the visual cue until the child is able to perform the task independently. Providing suggestions for *modeling* (demonstrating) skills to the student is also another important component of teaching early numeracy to children with developmental disabilities. Chapter 6 describes prompting and prompt fading techniques in more detail.

Specification of a clear mastery criterion

Regardless of how teaching objectives have been initially described, they also need to be written in such a way that teachers can clearly identify when the objectives have been met. That is, the goals for learning should be clearly defined so that they are observable and measurable. They should also include an accuracy criterion so that teachers can objectively know when a teaching goal has been achieved. Therefore, in the lesson plans that accompany this book we also specify a clear *mastery criterion*. We consider mastery of a skill as the ability of a student to respond immediately to the teacher's question for three consecutive correct responses (the first time they are asked on a given day). The students would need to demonstrate this mastery before moving on to learning the next skill in the sequence. In Chapter 8, a record keeping or *data collection* system is described that teachers can use to monitor a student's progress so they know when a skill is mastered and the student is ready to move on to the next learning objective or, alternatively, when a student needs additional help. The data collection system involves a minimum of paperwork so that little time is taken from actual teaching.

Specification of generalization strategies

As described in Chapter 2, a key component of constructivist theory is that learning should be meaningful and related to real-life situations. This is similar to the idea from Systematic Instruction that learners should have specific practice with *generalization* if learning is to occur. This is particularly important for many children with autism who may excessively adhere to ritualized patterns of behavior and are resistant to change (American Psychiatric Association, 2013). In a mathematical context, this might mean that a child is only able to respond if an instruction is given in a specific word format, if they work with the class teacher but not with a different staff member, or if they expect teaching stimuli to always be the same. Generalization cannot be expected to just happen, but should always be planned systematically (Baer et al., 1968). Promoting generalization should, therefore, be an important part of any teaching approach (Anderson & Romanczyk, 1999), particularly for children with autism.

To take this into account, we have added generalization suggestions to every lesson plan. This specification will help to ensure that students generalize skills across different environments (e.g., counting number of steps in the playground, in the classroom and in the dinner hall), with a variety of materials (e.g., counting plastic counters, books, pens) or with different teachers (e.g., the class teacher, teaching assistants or even demonstrating the skill to peers). For the earlier example of making and counting sequences of hand-chopping movements (see lesson plan A6.1: Copying and Counting Temporal Sequences of Movements), generalization suggestions include asking the child to make a sequence of sounds using a tambourine or a play hammer, and performing the task with different staff members. Teachers are further advised that students should not move on to the next teaching activity in the hierarchical sequence of skills until generalization of each specific skill has occurred (see Chapter 7).

Adapting the Mathematics Recovery teaching approach

Initial assessment

One modification to the Mathematics Recovery teaching approach involves how the student's levels of numeracy skills are assessed on the different domains (2A, 2B and 2C) prior to them starting the teaching program. With neurotypical children, an assessment interview would normally be conducted during which the teacher would ask the student to describe their strategies for solving a task. Because the level of language used in such an interview can be too complex for many students with a developmental disability (e.g., asking the student to describe a method they used to solve a task), in the approach set out in this book, we recommend substituting the interview with probes (test questions) corresponding to the individual numeracy skills, using simpler, more succinct instructions. A teacher who knows the student well is usually able to decide at which developmental Mathematics Recovery stage the child should be tested (Emergent, Perceptual or Figurative), although sometimes a student may need to be tested across stages.

In a probing (testing) session, the student is asked two questions initially corresponding to each skill. If the student answers both questions correctly, the skill is considered known by the student, whereas if two wrong answers are given the skill is considered not known and the student would need to be taught that skill. In the case of one correct and one wrong answer, a third question is asked. If the student answers correctly, the skill is considered known, otherwise it has to be taught. The purpose of these probing sessions is to help determine which skills need to be taught to the student. This initial assessment procedure is described in full in Chapter 8.

Increasing motivation for learning

A lack of motivation for engagement with academic tasks in the classroom has often been associated with a developmental disability, including autism. What motivates most neurotypical children (i.e., receiving praise from their parents or teachers, or gaining satisfaction from their problem-solving activities and successfully completing a task) does not always impact on the learning of children with a developmental disability. Having procedures in place to increase motivation, such as the use of rewards based on the student's interests, is an important component of the approach set out in this book. To sustain motivation to work through new, difficult tasks, instructions for differential reinforcement are described. For example, unprompted correct answers may be rewarded with tokens which can later be exchanged for a favorite activity. If a child needs help, however, they may be praised for answers following a prompt, but with tokens only delivered for unprompted correct responses. Strategies for motivating students with a developmental disability to learn are described in Chapter 4.

Repeated practice

Students with a developmental disability are believed to benefit from repeated practice because of their memory problems and difficulty in processing information (e.g., Swanson & Sachse-Lee, 2000). Providing numerous and repeated practice opportunities for children to enable them to strongly master skills and knowledge at each step in the curriculum is a key component of our approach and is consistent with the rehearsal mode of Mathematics Recovery described in Chapter 2 of the red book. Repeated practice can be achieved through following a *discrete-trial teaching* approach (described in Chapter 5).

When used appropriately, repeated practice can be an extremely powerful instructional tool that not only helps students learn and retain basic skills and facts in a fluent fashion, but may also have positive outcomes when students need to attempt to learn higher-order strategies. As Heward (2003) points out, the ability to use basic skills in mathematics without having to stop and think about them, which can be achieved through numerous and repeated practice opportunities, allows students to focus more of their attention on solving more complex tasks. For example, if students are not fluent in basic number facts, then their ability to solve more complex arithmetic tasks may be hindered: they must use their working memory to remember basic number facts, and thus will have less attention to focus on a problem-solving aspect of a task. It is possible that through the repeated practice of basic skills initially, children will then be better able to engage in the higher levels of critical or abstract thinking skills required for enquiry-based learning to occur.

Fast-paced sessions, with monitoring and feedback

Another element of the teaching approach set out in this book, appropriate for students with a developmental disability, is the use of fast-paced lessons with monitoring and feedback. This can also be achieved by following a discrete-trial teaching approach, described in Chapter 5. Each discrete trial comprises three components: the teacher's instruction to the child, the student's response which can be prompted by the teacher if necessary, and finally the teacher providing feedback and some type of reward if the child is correct, for example by providing a high-five, praise, a short interval of playing with a toy, or a token which can later be exchanged for a favorite activity. When the student is unable to complete a task, the teacher might present the same task again with a prompt, thus partially helping the student to respond. This is an example of an *error correction* procedure, described in Chapter 6. There are some similarities between error correction and the key instructional element, *Scaffolding during solving a task*, from Mathematics Recovery (e.g., see p. 98 of the white book).

During discrete-trial teaching, the students are able to respond as rapidly and as frequently as they are able during at least some fast-paced teaching sessions each day. Providing between 10 and 15 responses per minute is not unusual. As discrete-trial teaching allows for a fast pace of teaching, it provides many opportunities for children to work on their numeracy targets in each teaching session.

Research evidence for *Teaching Early Numeracy to Children with Developmental Disabilities*

The initial development of *Teaching Early Numeracy to Children with Developmental Disabilities* began in 2005–9 in North Wales, UK. Mathematics Recovery was already being implemented with neurotypical children in a mainstream school in Flintshire, North Wales, but we wanted to see if it could be used with children who attended an autism unit in the same school. The primary aim of the initial investigation was to examine the feasibility of adapting the Mathematics Recovery program for use with children with autism.

To ensure a consistent approach to teaching (i.e., fidelity of implementation), we developed a detailed teaching manual, which described many of the adaptations summarized above. An additional aim of our first study was to investigate whether intensive individualized teaching using Mathematics Recovery could improve the numeracy skills of children with autism who received the intervention and whether any gains that children made after the intervention were maintained over time.

In this early evaluation, six children with autism participated and received daily numeracy teaching, delivered by their regular teachers, over a 20-week period (Tzanakaki et al., 2014a). We found that it was easy to incorporate the program into each child's daily teaching timetable, and that all six children improved their mathematical ability over the course of the intervention and that these skills were maintained after a period of no intervention (approximately six weeks). The study also highlighted that the adapted Mathematics Recovery teaching manual was a tool that could be used to teach early numeracy to children with autism across very different levels of ability. Some of the children had very little spoken language or non-existent numeracy skills. However, all of them were able to access the curriculum.

Given the positive outcomes from this development and feasibility project, we decided to more fully evaluate the adapted Mathematics Recovery (*Teaching Early Numeracy to Children with Developmental Disabilities*) intervention. In our next study, we extended our previous research by using the approach with children with severe developmental disabilities, who did not necessarily have autism, and who attended a large special school in North Wales (Tzanakaki et al., 2014b). We adopted a stronger experimental design and a larger number of participants than we did in the initial autism research. We also employed a waiting list control group design and compared the progress of a group of children who were taught individually with *Teaching Early Numeracy to Children with Developmental Disabilities* to that of a similar group of children who received 'mathematics as usual' teaching within the same school setting. Twenty-four elementary school children with severe developmental disabilities or autism were randomly allocated to the intervention and control groups. Teachers and paraprofessionals in the school were trained to deliver the program.

Our initial intent was for every child in the intervention group to have four to five intervention sessions per week over a 12-week period. However, this did not prove to be possible in practice. Some of the children had as few as 13 individualized sessions in total, whereas others had over 30 teaching sessions over the course of the study. Sessions typically lasted between 15 and 20 minutes. Thus, for 12 weeks, one to three times a week, the 12 children in the intervention group received our program, while those in the control group received 'mathematics as usual' teaching. Pre- and post-intervention tests on standardized numeracy measures were conducted. Analysis of data from outcome measures indicated that the children in the intervention group made greater improvements at post-intervention in comparison to the children in the control group. A follow-up test showed that gains were maintained seven months after the end of the intervention.

Despite these positive outcomes, as mentioned previously, teachers and paraprofessionals found it difficult to adhere to the proposed level of intervention intensity (four to five sessions per week) and the researchers conducting the study needed to take on some of the direct teaching so that the children continued to receive their sessions for the period of the study. In a large special needs school setting, events such as school outings, staff training sessions, or a child in the classroom requiring extra attention often resulted in the teaching assistants being unable to find the necessary time to implement the intervention, especially as a 1:1 staff–student ratio was required for implementation.

Earlier versions of the *Teaching Early Numeracy to Children with Developmental Disabilities* lesson plans were also translated into Norwegian. Five children from a primary school in Norway received the intervention and its effects were evaluated (Tryggestad & Eldevik 2016). One child had developmental disabilities and another had been diagnosed with Asperger's Syndrome. All children were underperforming in mathematics. In this study, all children received the intervention for a total of 30 sessions across six weeks, each session lasting 30 minutes. The study was intended to be a systematic replication of the Tzanakaki et al. (2014b) study that had examined the effects of *Teaching Early Numeracy to Children with Developmental Disabilities* in the UK. Results were encouraging, with moderate to large effect sizes measured by standardized tests of mathematics. Following the Norwegian version of the numeracy program, the students gained an average of eight months of mathematical age after the six-week intervention.

In the studies described thus far, the numeracy program was delivered to the students at least some of the time by specialists in Systematic Instruction procedures (often the researchers themselves). Thus, although these studies have something interesting to say about the efficacy of the program (i.e., that it *can* be effective when delivered by experts in the intervention and when the students receive individualized instruction), they say very little about the effectiveness of *Teaching Early Numeracy to Children with Developmental Disabilities* (i.e., can it still be effective when delivered all the time by everyday staff in school settings who are not experts in delivering Systematic Instruction?).

To explore this effectiveness question, Apanasionok et al. (2020) recruited 17 students with autism from a large special school for children with severe developmental disabilities in the UK. Twelve staff members (five class teachers and seven paraprofessionals) across five classes were trained at the start of the study, using the approach described in this book. Researchers also supported staff in delivering the intervention via feedback provided following regular class visits and observations.

The proposed level of intensity of the *Teaching Early Numeracy to Children with Developmental Disabilities* intervention for one school year was for all students to have the opportunity to practice multiple times six current targets at least three times a week, with an additional session focused on generalization of skills (usually in a whole class teaching scenario). The teaching sessions were implemented using a delivery model frequently employed across the school. The students sat at a table in small groups of two or three with one member of staff (a class teacher or paraprofessional). Teachers delivered instruction for a few minutes to one student at a time, while the remaining students in the group accessed a reward for previously completed work or an independent activity. After a few trials (teachers gauged how long to work with individual students), the student receiving the instruction was given a reward to engage with or an independent activity and the teacher moved on to the next student. This process was repeated for 45 minutes or until the teacher decided that all students in the group had received sufficient practice on all six of their current targets. This delivery model helped to overcome the practical problems identified in the previous studies where an individual staff member was always required to work with just one student at a time. This was not always possible as teachers often had professional responsibilities elsewhere.

A standardized test for numeracy (the TEMA-3; Test of Early Mathematics Ability, 3rd edition) was conducted on all children at two time points: once immediately prior to the start of the intervention (baseline), and again at the end of the first school year (Time 1). All children improved their TEMA-3 raw scores at post-test compared to pre-test (with large effect size pre-post group difference), and 14 students' age-equivalent scores also improved after accessing the program for one school year.

Immediately after Time 1, 10 teachers who had been delivering the intervention for the year were interviewed using a semi-structured format about their experiences and perceptions of the intervention. Alallawi et al. (2020a) reported that taking part in *Teaching Early Numeracy to Children with Developmental Disabilities* was perceived as being a valuable experience for both the educators and their students. Although there was initial skepticism about the intervention prior to starting, this transferred to conviction over the implementation period. One teacher explained, 'I've worked with two different sets of staff with doing this kind of approach of teaching … initially all of them were a bit like "uh, it's repetitive" but all of them now prefer it, because they see the difference that it makes'.

Teachers were also impressed with how much their students had progressed, having initially thought that their students did not have the ability to learn new numeracy skills and, consequently, had not tried to teach them. As one teacher explained, 'when they know how to count, and they recognize numbers, I was amazed to see … they are able to do it and we didn't give them the chance to do that'. Another teacher added, 'Like the domino cards with the air, doing pattern – it's almost there but that we never thought they'll be able to do.' A further teacher commented, 'When you actually see the difference it makes and the progress the student can make with this kind of approach – it changes your opinions.'

Teachers also reported an increased sense of competence in their teaching skills, which was evident in greater satisfaction and increased self-efficacy. For example, one teacher commented, 'It's certainly giving me more confidence teaching mathematics. I struggle with mathematics, I had to work hard in school so, yes, it's good and it's certainly simplified things that are worrying for a teacher.' Another explained, 'I learnt more about mathematics. I never had a strong suit, in terms of teaching it before, but with the [TEN-DD] I feel like I have more solid understanding of what they (the children) could be.'

Finally, there was strong interest in continuing to use *Teaching Early Numeracy to Children with Developmental Disabilities* with the students beyond the study period as well as in the importance of the numeracy program being made available for other students. One teacher recalled a discussion with a parent of an 18-year-old pupil with severe developmental disabilities whom he taught when he was 13–14 years old: 'I spoke to a parent of a child I used to teach, and he still hasn't learnt how to count, and he can't do the course that they want in a college because he can't count, whereas if he had something like this, and he doesn't like to count now because he thinks he can't do it – so if he had that intervention earlier then I think it would have benefited him.'

Training and involving parents to support their child's mathematical development also potentially increases the number of children who might benefit from *Teaching Early Numeracy to Children with Developmental Disabilities*, and is also valued in policy (e.g., Education Endowment Foundation, 2016). Alallawi et al. (2020b) carried out an initial evaluation of using this approach with three Arabic children with autism by training and supporting their parents to deliver the intervention for an eight-week period. For this study, lesson plans were also translated into Arabic. Using a pre-test post-test design, results from a standardized assessment revealed that the three children's mathematical ability improved over the course of the intervention. Parents also described positive experiences of their training and of using the approach, especially mentioning how much their children had progressed in their understanding of mathematics. The study data show promising results and provide initial evidence that *Teaching Early Numeracy to Children with Developmental Disabilities* can be adapted for parents to use in a home context.

4

Motivating students with developmental disabilities to learn

Asim's story: Instructional protocol for teaching identification of numeral 21

Asim is a 10-year-old boy with autism who attends a special school for children with a moderate intellectual disability. He receives mathematics teaching sessions three times a week for about 20 minutes at a time. He has been assessed for his numeracy skill development and a number of learning objectives have been specified for him. One of his targets is to learn how to identify the numeral 21 (i.e., when he is asked, 'what number is this?' that he can say, '21'). Asim can already identify numerals 1–20 but has not yet learnt how to label numerals 21–30. To make the task easier for Asim, as he has never before correctly said '21' when he has seen the numeral 21, his teacher holds up the numeral card and models saying the words 'twenty-one'. When Asim correctly repeats the words, he is praised enthusiastically and is given a small square picture of his favorite character (Lego Batman) to place on a 10-item token strip. Asim had already learnt that when he receives his 10 tokens, he can exchange the tokens for a preferred item or activity. Immediately prior to his numeracy session, Asim was given five choices to select from that he could earn during the session (he had selected a picture of the Batman Lego movie icon to

(Continued)

indicate that this was what he wanted to work toward). Over four instructional attempts, the teacher models less of the word: first, she says 'twenty-one', then she says 'twenty "w"...', then she says 'twenty...' (and raises her eyebrows and looks expectantly at him), and finally she holds up the numeral card and asks, 'what number?' and Asim correctly says 'twenty-one'. To be sure that Asim has attended to the word and is not responding simply because of the verbal model he has received on the previous attempts, the teacher switches tasks and asks Asim to follow some simple directions regarding touching body parts that he has learnt. The teacher then returns to present the numeral card 21 for Asim to identify. Asim says 'twenty-one' correctly. Asim is praised profusely and is given his last token to place on the board. He takes off the Lego Batman picture and hands it, laughing, to his teacher. They watch the Lego movie clip on the tablet together and chat about what they are watching.

Curriculum has been defined as the 'what' of teaching, and instruction (or pedagogy) as the 'how' of teaching (e.g., Sands et al., 2000). The previous example, to illustrate Asim learning to identify the numeral card 21, describes how he is being taught. The 'what' of his teaching (the curriculum) includes the instructional objective that this program is addressing (learning to identify numeral 21) as well as the prerequisite targets that led to that current step (e.g., learning to identify numerals 1–20) and the future targets that will be taught once he has learnt to identify numeral 21 correctly (e.g., learning numerals 22–30). The 'what' of teaching for *Teaching Early Numeracy to Children with Developmental Disabilities* (in the form of lesson plans) can be downloaded from the website accompanying this book.

The 'how' of teaching can be compartmentalized into some key features of the instructional elements illustrated in the above example. When the teacher asks the question, 'What number?', waits for a response and then praises enthusiastically when Asim provides the correct answer, this is an example of discrete-trial teaching. The teacher's use of a verbal model by saying 'twenty-one' is an example of a prompt. Asim was assisted in identifying the numeral correctly with an additional cue that he had already learnt how to use (i.e., he had already learnt how to verbally echo words). Over time, the verbal prompt was gradually removed as Asim continued to identify the numeral correctly. This is referred to as prompt fading. Another example of teaching illustrated in the example was the use of a reinforcer. If a response is correct, the student receives a preferred object or activity that increases the likelihood that they will use that same response in the future. Asim received praise for correct responding, but also small pictures of Lego Batman that were later exchanged for a previously selected delayed reinforcer (getting to watch the trailer for the Lego Batman movie). He had previously selected the Lego Batman trailer to work for during a reinforcer preference assessment procedure. After Asim had answered correctly without a verbal prompt, his teacher switched to an alternative task and then returned to the numeral identification task. This is an example of using distraction and retesting to see if the student can still remember.

These key instructional elements summarized in Asim's story, the 'how' of teaching early numeracy to children with developmental disabilities, will be described in detail in Chapters 4–8. In this chapter, we will describe how you can improve students' motivation for learning during teaching sessions. We will introduce the topics of operant learning and reinforcement and you will learn how to identify reinforcers for the students you work with, and how to establish and use token reinforcement systems. In Chapter 5, we address the question: what is discrete-trial teaching, and how can it be delivered effectively? In Chapter 6, we will describe prompting and prompt fading procedures and you will also learn what to do when a student makes a mistake and how to correct errors effectively. In Chapter 7, we will describe how you can help the student to use the mathematical skills learnt in structured sessions in a variety of different settings, with different people, and across time. Chapter 7 also focuses on providing practical suggestions for including maintenance and generalization in your instruction. Chapter 8 provides an overview of the lesson plans supplied with this book and how they can be used, as well as describing how to assess the student so that you know exactly which areas should be the first to teach.

Principles of teaching and learning for children with developmental disabilities

Many of the teaching strategies you will be reading about in this book are based on Applied Behavior Analysis, which is often abbreviated to ABA. Applied Behavior Analysis is based on the work of the American psychologist B. F. Skinner, who concerned himself with studying behavior and the process of learning (e.g., Skinner, 1968). ABA takes the findings of Skinner and his followers and applies these findings to human beings in a variety of settings such as hospitals, workplaces, homes and schools.

What is Applied Behavior Analysis?

Applied Behavior Analysis is an approach to learning that employs scientifically proven principles of learning to help bring about positive changes for a person. There are three important characteristics of ABA. First, for teachers, the behaviors that you will want to be teaching are behaviors that will have important real-life implications for the student you are working with (these are sometimes called socially significant behaviors). This is the 'applied' part in Applied Behavior Analysis. For an intervention to be applied, it should also be aiming to produce behavioral changes that will produce long-term benefits for the individual concerned. Using this terminology, the approach outlined in this book can undoubtedly be thought of as an applied educational approach, because we are concerned with how the principles of ABA can be used to help teach mathematical skills to students with developmental disabilities, that ultimately will help to bring about long-term functional benefits for them.

Second, in ABA, we are working with real, observable, measurable behaviors, rather than some abstract inference of behavior. This is the 'behavior' part in Applied Behavior Analysis. A behavior could be anything a person does. From a mathematics point of view, it could be saying the forward number word sequence from 1 to 10, writing down answers to single-digit addition sums, counting the number of claps that a teacher makes, and so on. What is crucial though is that a target behavior can be operationally defined, is clearly observable (seen, heard, etc.) and can be measured (e.g., counted) in a variety of ways that we will describe later in Chapter 8.

We are concerned with objective behaviors that can be measured, not just a subjective personal opinion about a behavior that cannot be precisely measured. If a teacher describes a student as being 'anxious' about their mathematics work without exactly specifying their behaviors, we have no way of knowing exactly what they observed that may have led them to this conclusion, or what exactly the student did. Feeling anxious, for example, could describe many different behaviors ranging from 'asking teachers for help at least three times during a five-minute mathematics exercise' or 'finishing a mathematics task at least five minutes slower than the rest of the class'. We need this more precise objective information about a student's mathematical behaviors so that we can work out more clearly what exactly should be done to rectify any problem. We can also then be more certain that any help we provide is having the hoped-for effect and is helping the student.

The third and final characteristic of ABA is, regarding an intervention or educational plan, that any decision regarding what to do next should always be based on objective data collection from direct observation and monitoring of a person's progress. Data collection methods can help us understand what effect, if any, the teaching being used is having on the behavior. This is the analysis part. For the teaching of mathematics, this is important because it allows teachers to be able to see quickly whether a particular teaching strategy is working. Often, this decision can be reached much more quickly using data collection methods than if a teacher is relying on their own feeling about the effectiveness of their teaching. If teachers are keeping a close watch over what is happening with the student's learning using data collection methods, then they can quickly make adjustments and revise their teaching as needed. This helps to ensure each child's ongoing progress. Data collection methods will be described in more detail in Chapter 8.

Teaching Early Numeracy to Children with Developmental Disabilities is an approach that is grounded in behavioral science. This book is our attempt at distilling this broad framework into simple processes that teachers can easily understand and apply to their teaching. The book, as a whole, will exemplify this; but in this chapter we want to explain a key process that we consider to be the pillar of effective teaching: operant learning. Operant principles are essential for understanding how we teach new skills to children through using positive reinforcement, **so** we will also focus on explaining how you can identify and use positive reinforcement effectively with the students with whom you work.

What is operant learning?

In using behavioral approaches, it is of course very important that we pay close attention to the skills (behaviors) that we want to teach. However, in ABA there are other factors that are important to consider too, especially what happens before a behavior occurs, usually called the antecedent, and the events that happen after a behavior occurs, usually called the consequence. These three components, often referred to as the ABCs of behavior, are crucial to understand if we are to know how to effectively teach students. In fact, the relationship between these three elements is so important that Skinner came up with a special term to describe it, called the Contingency of Reinforcement. There are three parts to this concept: '(1) an occasion upon which behavior occurs, (2) the behavior itself, and (3) the consequences of the behavior' (Skinner, 1968, p. 4). This is also sometimes called the three-term contingency.

When we talk of consequences, we are usually talking about what happens immediately after a behavior occurs. Things that follow a behavior with a certain degree of regularity often begin to have an effect on how frequently the behavior that they follow occurs. The process through which these consequences influence behavior is called operant learning. For example, if a young girl is being potty trained and is given a small toy to play with each time that she uses the potty, and we see that she starts to use the potty more frequently instead of having an accident, then that toy can be said to be a positive reinforcer for using the potty. The toy is said to be 'reinforcing' the hoped-for outcome of the girl starting to use the potty more. However, if the same girl does not use the potty more often despite being given the toy, then we could *not* say that that same toy is a positive reinforcer as it is not increasing the frequency of the girl using the potty. A different preferred item could be tried as a reward; perhaps a chocolate button each time she uses the potty.

Generally speaking, if something that a student likes follows one of their behaviors (for example, in mathematics a teacher saying 'well done' and giving a high-five after the student has correctly counted in 10s to 100), it is probably safe to say that their behavior has been reinforced and they would be a bit more likely to remember to repeat that same behavior a second time to receive the reinforcer again (in this case, the teacher saying 'well done' and giving a high-five). However, if something that the student does not like follows a behavior (for example, the teacher frowning when the student answers in a particular way or saying, 'No, that's not right'), then they would probably be less likely to give that same answer on another occasion.

Operant learning is the most common of the various ways in which learning is believed to take place and is the underlying principle of most of the behavior change techniques used in ABA. Operant learning has the most relevance for the strategies described in this book. There are many similarities between the operant learning model associated with Skinner, and our everyday understanding of motivation. To understand the operant learning model in terms of motivation, the likelihood of the behavior occurring can be thought of as the motivation and the reinforcement as the motivator. To use the earlier example, the likelihood of the girl using the potty (her motivation to do so) is increasing because of the toy she receives (the motivator).

Understanding motivation for learning and teaching

Motivation (from the Latin *movere* meaning 'to move') can be defined as 'the reason why somebody does something or behaves in a particular way' (Oxford Learner's Dictionary, 2020). Motivation is what causes us to behave, whether it is reaching out our hand to pick up a glass of water (we are motivated by our thirst) or reading a book (we are motivated by our desire to gain knowledge, or to enjoy a story). One of the most powerful and effective methods to increase motivation is positive reinforcement. Technically speaking, positive reinforcement involves the addition of a reinforcing stimulus following a behavior that makes it more likely that the behavior will occur again in the future. When the stimulus is desirable or pleasant, the positive reinforcer is often called a reward. In this book, we will use the terms positive reinforcer and reward interchangeably. Whether you are using positive reinforcement with the children you work with to encourage good work or on yourself to work toward personal goals, it can provide the boost of motivation needed to reach goals that have been decided upon.

We all respond to positive reinforcement, whether it is the pay check we receive at the end of the working month or the free coffee we get when we have amassed our 10 loyalty stamps from a café. Children with a developmental disability are no different. They will also respond in a positive way when they are rewarded for certain behaviors. They will continue to do more of a behavior to receive a positive reward. Effective use of positive reinforcers is probably the most powerful tool as a teacher you will ever have at your disposal to help motivate a child with a developmental disability to learn new skills. However, we often hear teachers say such things as 'Donald should just be happy to get on with his work' or 'Sarah should not need any rewards, she just needs to learn to do what she is told'. We believe that there are three main reasons why people may object to the use of reinforcers (motivators) with children with a developmental disability and these are summarized in Table 4.1 and described in more detail below.

Table 4.1 Common objections to the use of reinforcers with children with a developmental disability

1.	Using reinforcement is no better than bribery
2.	The child's learning will become dependent on receiving rewards
3.	It is too hard to find any reinforcers to motivate the child

Common objections to using reinforcers with children with a developmental disability

Using reinforcement is no better than bribery

Many people feel that using reinforcers with children is not a natural thing to do, and that the decision to use them is too arbitrary. These apprehensions often stem from having seen reinforcers being used incorrectly with no plan for fading their use. Criticisms also often stem from the belief that using rewards is no better than 'bribery'. Contrary to popular belief, bribery is not the same as using positive reinforcement. Bribery is when a teacher negotiates a reward for a student's cooperation after they have refused to do a task. Bribery is telling a child who is being disruptive when they are presented with a mathematics task that they will receive a reward if they stop ('If you stop screaming, you can go in the playground to calm down'). The child stops screaming and gets to go in the playground without completing their mathematics task.

If you remind the student of what they can get *after* a demonstration of challenging behavior, this will most likely increase the chances of challenging behavior occurring in the future in similar situations. The main difference between bribery and reinforcement is that with bribery the item that the child wants comes *before* they have engaged in the appropriate behavior. They are given what they want and then they may promise to do their work after. With positive reinforcement, on the other hand, the reinforcer is only delivered *after* the child has engaged in the expected behavior.

The child's learning will become dependent on receiving rewards

Concerns about the use of positive reinforcement are also frequently broached based on the belief that the student will become dependent on rewards, and that the student will not do their work in school unless they receive frequent reinforcement. This is a fair criticism, but it is valid only if reinforcers are not faded or reduced properly. Chapter 5 on discrete-trial teaching and Chapter 7 on generalization provide some guidance on how to do this effectively.

It is too hard to find any reinforcers to motivate the child

Another reason why teachers sometimes say that they do not use reinforcement with a child is that they have struggled to find anything that is sufficiently powerful to motivate them. Many children with developmental disabilities can appear demotivated during many academic learning tasks, including those involving mathematics. One of the issues is that for many children with a developmental disability, the sorts of social consequences that usually motivate neurotypical children, such as receiving praise from their parents and teachers, imitating peers, and successfully completing a task, are not impactful on the behavior of a child with a developmental disability. They often have a long history of failure, criticism, and low expectations from others and so it is not surprising that these children can appear demotivated.

Most of us can remember times when we received praise in our lives. If you think back to those occasions when somebody praised you (positive social reinforcement), you will probably appreciate that after you had received the praise it made you want to, at the very least, continue to do what you did before, or maybe it made you want to strive to work even harder in the future or perform even better, or at least continue to do as well as you were doing before. Praise is ubiquitous, strengthening children's behaviors in classrooms everywhere. For children with a developmental disability, however, if praise does not function to strengthen (reinforce) the behaviors that we would like to see more of, what can we do? We need to understand that everybody needs reinforcers of some description to motivate their behavior and that children with a developmental disability are no exception. If children with a developmental disability are not currently motivated by the sorts of things that motivate other children, we may need to be a bit more creative about finding out what reinforcers work best for them.

Identifying reinforcers for a child with a developmental disability is not as straightforward as it may first appear. Sometimes children have lots of preferred items freely available and they are rarely expected to work for these. If eating preferred snacks, playing video games, or playing with preferred toys is frequently allowed anyway, the items or activities will not usually function as a reinforcer under these circumstances because they will not increase the behaviors they follow. We can also use the strategies described in the 'Identifying reinforcers' section below. In fact, even if you think you can easily identify some potential rewards for a child you work with, you need to bear in mind that the child may quickly become bored with the rewards if you use them too often. For this reason, it is always worthwhile to continuously try to identify and develop new reinforcers for any child that you work with.

There can be lots of different kinds of reinforcers, and the terminology used to describe them can be confusing. In the section below, we explain some of the most common terms. You will see these terms used throughout the book.

Types of reinforcers

Intrinsic reinforcer

Sometimes the act of doing something may be enjoyable in itself. If this is the case, we say that the activity is intrinsically reinforcing or that it is an intrinsic reinforcer. For some children, playing a musical instrument, drawing, or reading stories might be said to be intrinsically reinforcing if they enjoy doing these activities anyway and if there is no need for any artificial consequences to encourage them to participate. It cannot be presumed that all children will find mathematics tasks intrinsically reinforcing, although this is the hoped-for outcome in Mathematics Recovery (see e.g., p. 30 in the green book).

Extrinsic reinforcer

Extrinsic reinforcers are those that we can usually see, feel, touch and so on, such as small toys that a child might like to play with, or being given a small sweet after working well. Extrinsic reinforcers have an arbitrary relationship to the behaviors that lead to them (as when a musician plays for money rather than because they enjoy the music that the playing produces, as would be the case with an intrinsic reinforcer).

Food and drink are examples of extrinsic reinforcers that are also called primary reinforcers. Primary reinforcers are reinforcing in themselves and are often referred to as things that are needed to keep us alive. When a bit of food is used as a reinforcer, it is often called an edible reinforcer. Small pieces of food, such as grapes, chocolate buttons, small sweets and the like can be used as edible reinforcers. Whether or not to use food or drink as a reinforcer is a very contentious issue. Understandably, many professionals and parents balk at the very idea of feeding a child with tiny bits of food throughout the day to motivate them to learn. Some people complain, 'it is no better than dog training'; others wonder why children should be being rewarded with food for what can often be very small tasks that appear to take little effort. These are valid concerns. We should of course worry about the health implications, such as tooth decay and potential weight gain, if children are given chocolate and sweets frequently throughout the day. There is, however, a balance to consider. In our work with children with a developmental disability, which spans several decades, we have come across hundreds of children who are not able to respond positively to praise in the beginning of teaching, or who have very few reinforcers that are powerful enough to increase the frequency of the behavior that they come after. The child is stuck in limbo with their learning, failing to learn any new skills, all because of a failure to find and use effective reinforcers to motivate them to engage in learning activities. Sometimes, primary reinforcers in the form of food are the only things that teachers have available to them that will be effective. You may want to consider using edible reinforcers with a child you work with if any of the following situations occur: (1) the child struggles to learn any new skills; (2) there are very few learning activities that the child will willingly participate in without engaging in challenging behavior; or (3) you have very few items or activities that you could potentially use as a reinforcer.

If you do decide to use primary or edible reinforcers, there are some cautions regarding their use. The plan should always be to keep the bites of an edible reinforcer small so that they do not add up to much food across the day. One teacher we have worked with used to cut Smarties into eight pieces and use one piece at a time as a reinforcer. If you are using drink as a reinforcer, the child should be provided with small sips across the day, or if juice is being used, try using juice diluted with water. Remember too that using edibles is only ever intended to be a temporary solution, used until such time that they can be replaced by other social reinforcers like praise or other, more natural reinforcers. Toward this aim, you should always praise the child at the same time as giving them the edible reinforcer. In time, you would hope that the praise (i.e., a social reinforcer) takes on reinforcing value of its own by this pairing. This idea of pairing is discussed in more detail in Chapter 5 on discrete-trial teaching and Chapter 7 on generalization.

Another powerful extrinsic reinforcer for many children is watching video clips either on television, computer screens, or hand-held devices. Many of the children we teach are extremely motivated to watch their favorite shows, music videos, film trailers, or comedy clips. Figuring out the best reward system for a child will help them learn mathematics, even if you are initially having to use sweets and time watching videos to motivate them. As with the edible reinforcers, watching any video clips should really only be permitted in small amounts. For example, if a child has just managed a few minutes of focused engaged work you could reinforce their work with watching their favorite video clip for 30 seconds or so.

Another term that you may hear in relation to using extrinsic reinforcers is conditioned reinforcement or secondary reinforcement. These reinforcers are not inherently reinforcing by themselves (like food or drink), but they may begin to work as reinforcers after they become associated with primary reinforcers (or other already effective conditioned reinforcers) that often follow them. Above, we described how praise paired with edible items might work in this way. Stickers on a chart sometimes used in classrooms are also conditioned reinforcers. Token economies, built around using tokens and trading the tokens in for rewards and prizes, are another example of using conditioned reinforcers. These systems are highly effective at motivating children. Later in this chapter, you will be given instructions on how to set up a token economy system for the student you work with. The different types of reinforcers are summarized in Table 4.2.

Table 4.2 Summary of the types of reinforcers with definitions and examples of use

Reinforcer type	Definition and example of use
Intrinsic reinforcer	When a child engages in a behavior at a high rate in the absence of any observable external reinforcing consequence, engaging in the behavior by itself could be said to be functioning as an intrinsic reinforcer (or it is intrinsically motivating). Drawing, or reading stories may function as an intrinsic reinforcer for some children. Engaging in mathematics learning is not always intrinsically reinforcing for children with a developmental disability.
Extrinsic reinforcer	These can be observed (seen, heard, touched, etc.) and have an arbitrary relation to the behaviors they follow. A child may participate in numeracy lessons to start with to receive stickers (an example of being extrinsically motivated) rather than because they enjoy the feeling of accomplishment that engaging in numeracy tasks provides (an example of being intrinsically motivated).
Primary reinforcer	Primary reinforcers are reinforcing in themselves and are necessary to keep us alive. Food and drink are examples of primary reinforcers – reinforcing to everyone when we are hungry or thirsty.

Reinforcer type	Definition and example of use
Edible reinforcer	When a piece of food is used as a reinforcer, it is usually called an edible reinforcer (or an 'edible'). Small pieces of food can be used as an edible reinforcer. Using edibles should only ever be considered a temporary measure until such time that they can be replaced by social reinforcers (see below).
Conditioned reinforcer	Conditioned reinforcers are items or activities that initially are not reinforcing, but acquire reinforcing properties of their own over time through occurring simultaneously with (being paired with) primary reinforcers or other established conditioned reinforcers. Verbal praise, stickers, tokens, money and the like are examples of conditioned reinforcers.
Social reinforcer	A social reinforcer is a type of conditioned reinforcer that involves interaction from someone else. Verbal praise, smiles, acknowledgments, high-fives and the like are all examples of social reinforcers, providing that the child likes receiving this attention.

Identifying reinforcers

It is imperative that you identify powerful reinforcers for your student before you start their early numeracy program. To do this properly, you will need to individually determine reinforcers for all students that you work with. Not only do children's preferences change almost daily, but children can have very different individual likes and dislikes. It would be a mistake to presume that because one student you have worked with loved working for stickers that this will reinforce the behavior of another student. You should aim to compile a list of reinforcers for a student that is both varied and broad (consisting of 10–25 different potential items or activities). Information about preferences (reinforcers) for a student with a developmental disability can be gathered in four different ways:

1. Using interviews and surveys
2. Observing the student in their free time
3. Reinforcer sampling
4. Using preference assessments during teaching

Using interviews and surveys

One very simple way of finding out about the student's favorite activities, interests, things to eat, and so on, is to interview the student to ask what they like to do, or if they would find it difficult to answer, to ask other people such as their parents or teachers who know the student well. Asking sensory-related questions about what the student likes to see, hear, smell or touch can also be a useful source of potential reinforcers. The information can be obtained by asking open-ended questions (e.g., 'What does Henry like to do?', 'What does Matilda like to watch on TV?', 'What does Tom like to eat?') and then following this with comparison questions to find out the highest preferred items and activities (e.g., 'What does Tom like better, crisps or chocolate?', 'Would Henry rather play on the trampoline in the garden or go on the swing?').

Another way to find this information out is to use surveys or reinforcer inventories. A reinforcer inventory is a questionnaire or checklist that refers to items and experiences that may give a person joy or satisfaction. Usually there are a number of category headings of reinforcers (e.g., food items, toys and playthings, entertainment, sports and games) with specific items listed under each category. There is often a space for a teacher to rate on a scale how much the student enjoys the things described (e.g., from not at all, a little, to a fair amount, and very much). One widely used survey is the Reinforcement Assessment for Individuals with Severe Disabilities (RAISD; Fisher et al., 1996). This survey obtains information about potential reinforcers by asking a caregiver to write down answers to some questions that are focused primarily on finding out about sensory preferences (for example, 'Some individuals really enjoy different sounds such as listening to music, car sounds, whistles, beeps, sirens, clapping, people singing, etc. What are the things you think ____ most likes to listen to?'). There is also space to rank the potential reinforcers in order of preference. It is fairly easy to compile your own reinforcer inventory or survey and there are several examples on the internet to draw ideas from. You can also download an example of a reinforcer inventory from the website accompanying this book.

Observing the student in their free time

Another simple way to discover potential reinforcers is to observe the student to see what they like doing in their free time, and then to write down what the student appears to prefer doing. This process will help you to gain some understanding about what is intrinsically interesting and motivating to the student. If you are a teacher, it may be more difficult to gain these insights as there is not usually much free time in a school day and some activities would be more readily available in the home than at school. However, you may be able to send home to parents a list of questions structured in such a way as to find out about what the child likes to do in their free time at home (similar to the RAISD survey above, an example reinforcer sampling letter template is available on the website accompanying this book) and then you might be able to use some of these activities in school.

It may be that the student does not necessarily show much interest in the sorts of toys and activities that we would expect. Rather, there are specific items in the environment that they gravitate toward and seem to enjoy. Students with developmental disabilities may also like to watch certain things for long periods of time. Whirling fans or looking at wheels spinning are fairly common examples.

It can be useful to understand the precise aspect of behaviors a child engages in that they enjoy. Some children enjoy turning light switches on and off repeatedly. But what exactly is it about this that they are enjoying? Do they like the clicking noise that the switch makes as they move it up and down? Or is it the visual stimulation of the room going from light to dark and then back to light again? Perhaps they like the physical stimulation of pressing the switch up and down or maybe they like the response they get from the teacher when they play with the light switch ('Stop flicking the lights!'). For Josh, who liked climbing under tables, we discovered that he loved looking at right angles. Josh climbed under the tables to look closely at the right angle of the table leg abutting the top of the table. If the student likes watching videos, you may also want to try and find out exactly what it is about watching the video that the student finds enjoyable. It might not be immediately obvious. Try not to presume that the student would enjoy bits of the show that we would like or that most other students would like. Do they try to re-play a particular part again and again? We have worked with some students who appear to have little interest in the show itself, but who love just watching the rolling credits at the end of the show.

Why is it so important to try to find out the single most enjoyable characteristic of the student's preference, however unusual that might be? It can help to enhance their enjoyment of the activity and increase the likelihood that you will be able to use it as a powerful reinforcer. Importantly, however, it may also help you to identify other potential reinforcers based on that existing preference. That is, you may be able to transfer their sensory preference to other objects, activities, or actions. For Josh, who liked climbing under tables to look at table legs, we were able to transfer this preference to a wide range of materials that had right angles (e.g., from a mathematics geometry kit set) that he could play with at his table after completing learning activities (as reinforcers).

Reinforcer sampling

Another strategy to help find potential reinforcers for children is to carry out reinforcer sampling. This is when a child is presented with a sample of a potential reinforcer that they may never have experienced before so that they may gain some experience of the possible positive characteristics of that activity. Reinforcer sampling procedures emerged from the field of ABA over 50 years ago and are easy for teachers to use to develop new reinforcers for a child. For example, you may decide to play a novel board game with a student or bring in a new sticker book to see if they like collecting stickers to put in the book.

There are a few guidelines for conducting reinforcer sampling effectively. First of all, it is important to realize that when you are sampling potential reinforcers for the first time the student should not be having to 'earn' the opportunity to play or otherwise engage with the activity; rather, they should be allowed free access. Do not be surprised if the student seems fairly nonplussed the first time you present the activity. Many students can be won over and start to enjoy the activity you are sampling, provided you remember to introduce it in a fun and enthusiastic manner ('Wow, this is such a great game!'). Remember too that you may need to present an item or activity a few times for the student to start to enjoy it.

This is a well-known psychological phenomenon where people start to develop a preference for things because they are familiar with them.

Once you have sampled some items and activities a few times, it is a good idea to rate the student's enjoyment levels for each activity to help decide which to use (see also the 'Using interviews and surveys' section above, where rating the level of enjoyment is also recommended for reinforcer inventories). Sometimes, it can be helpful to categorize the ratings into a hierarchy of ABC reinforcers, or something similar. The A reinforcers would be those activities that the child liked the most. Make sure you put these aside and save for the most difficult-to-teach skills, or the time of day when the child needs a little bit more of a boost to be motivated to engage with your teaching. The B reinforcers would be those activities that the child liked a fair amount. You would want to use these for tasks of medium difficulty. The C-level reinforcers would be those activities that the child liked a little. You would use these items to reinforce fairly easy tasks. Brief instructions for reinforcer sampling and a reinforcer hierarchy form can be downloaded from the website accompanying this book.

Reinforcer sampling should be an ongoing process where you regularly try out new items and activities. All children can go through phases where they may absolutely love a particular toy, edible or TV show, but then it loses its appeal. You should constantly be on the lookout for the signs that children have lost interest and be ready to replace a reinforcer with something else that you have identified. Making reinforcer sampling a regular part of your teaching timetable can help to ensure that you have new, exciting items ready to use as soon as you need them.

Using preference assessments during teaching

Students will often vary in how they respond to different reinforcers for different tasks at different times. When you start teaching first thing in the morning, the student might really enjoy playing with a particular car as a reinforcer but by the time the afternoon comes round they may have lost interest. One way of being sure that the student is likely to be reinforced by an item or activity at any given time is to carry out a quick preference assessment, immediately prior to starting teaching. This involves presenting objects systematically to the student to reveal a hierarchy or a ranking of preferences.

There are many different preference assessment methods. A *single item preference assessment* is probably the quickest and the easiest method. Here, objects and activities are presented just one at a time and the student's reaction to the item is recorded, for example how long the student interacts with the object or activity. The item that the student engages with the longest is considered to be their most preferred item, which should then be able to be used as an effective reinforcer in the subsequent teaching session.

In the *paired item preference assessment* (sometimes called a 'forced choice'), the student is presented with two items at a time and asked to select one. When the student has selected each item, they are allowed to eat a small amount (if an edible reinforcer) or play with the toy for 30 seconds or so. One of the drawbacks of this procedure is that it takes a long time as each item has to be systematically paired with every other item in the set in a random order. The most frequently selected item from the pairings is considered to be the most potent reinforcer. Some researchers have found the paired method to be more accurate than the single item method (e.g., Pace et al., 1985; Paclawskyj & Vollmer, 1995). However, this advantage needs to be weighed up against the ease of use and simplicity of the single item preference assessment. There are different types of forms that have been recommended to record students' responses during preference assessments so that it is easy to work out which items are the most preferred. Examples of single item and paired item preference assessment data sheets can be downloaded from the website accompanying this book.

As can be seen, there are a number of different methods that can be used to help you find out what reinforcers will work best for the student you are working with. Without a powerful reinforcer, it is difficult to teach early numeracy to children with developmental disabilities effectively. Each method has its benefits and disadvantages, but using a combination of the different methods will be more beneficial than using one method only. In addition, preferences do change over time and require ongoing investigation. Therefore, identifying new potential reinforcers to use should be a routine part of your teaching. When selecting which method to use (interview, reinforcer inventory, observation, etc.), you will need to consider the amount of time you have available for the assessment, the types of preferred items and activities that are likely to be available and the student's communication level. Remember also that these reinforcer identification methods will only suggest *potential* reinforcers, not definite ones. You will only know for sure if something is functioning as a reinforcer if it *increases* behavior.

Using token economy systems

Many teachers who have gone through the program set out in this book have used token economy boards to help motivate their students. Under a token economy board system, the student can earn tokens through completing the mathematics tasks expected of them and can then later exchange these tokens for a highly valued reinforcer, such as a favorite food item, toy or activity. Tokens can be considered conditioned reinforcers, like money, that can be traded in or exchanged to obtain preferred items and activities. A token board then shows a student the main reinforcer they can obtain once a predetermined number of tokens have been earned.

Figure 4.1 shows an example of a token economy board where a student has to obtain 10 tokens to receive a reinforcer.

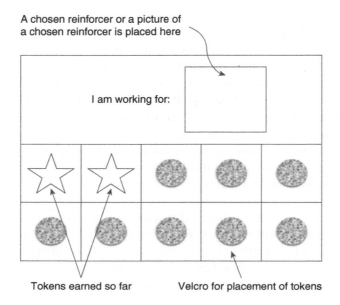

Figure 4.1   Example of a token economy board

Token economy boards are simple to use. When the student gives a desired response, the teacher gives the student a token to place on their token board. It can be beneficial to individualize the form of tokens for each student to reflect a special interest that they may have. In the earlier example, Asim loved the Lego Batman movie. Subsequently, pictures of Lego Batman were more appropriate to use for him than the more common tokens of stars or happy faces. The placement of the tokens can serve as a bridge between an expected response and the main reinforcer, and can help to maintain the student's motivation during learning tasks.

Steps in setting up a token economy system

1. Determine what items or activities will be motivating to the student using the methods described previously.
2. Make some pictures to represent these items or activities that can be placed on the space on the token board for the main reinforcer.
3. Decide on how many tokens need to be earned before gaining access to the main reinforcer. You may want to start by requiring only a small number of tokens (e.g., three to five) and gradually increase that number when appropriate.
4. Decide on the form of tokens to use. Ideally, they should be individualized and reflect one of the student's interests. You may also want to match these to the age and level

of the student. For example, for an older student it might be more appropriate to use coins, or a punch card.

5. Place a piece of Velcro behind each token so it can be secured to the token board.
6. Make the token board with spaces for:

    •   The tokens. In the example in Figure 4.1 there are spaces for 10 tokens, but it could be fewer.
    •   A picture of the main reinforcer or space for placing the main reinforcer if it is small (e.g., a chocolate button).

Implementing a token economy system

1. Remember, when introducing a token system, that this is a new tool for a student and will require a learning phase. Give the student frequent tokens at the beginning (even as much as one token per correct answer) so that there is frequent access to the reinforcer. When starting to use a token board with a student for the first time, you may want to start with a five-token board where you arrange that four of the five tokens are already placed on the board before you start teaching. The student then only needs to earn one token before they can receive the main reinforcer. Gradually increase the number of tokens required. For example, in the next step the student would have three tokens already placed and has to earn two, after this there would be two tokens already placed and they have to earn three, and so on until they have to earn all five tokens.
2. Always pair social praise with giving the tokens by saying, for example, 'well done', 'awesome work', or giving a high-five.
3. Once the student has learnt that tokens lead to the main reinforcer, you should be able to gradually lengthen the time between giving tokens, or increase the number of tokens required to obtain the main reinforcer.
4. Hand the token to the student. They should place it on the board themselves whenever possible, rather than the teacher doing it for them. This will ensure that they realise that they are receiving the reward because they responded correctly.
5. When the student has earned the predetermined number of tokens, encourage the student to take the picture of the main reinforcer off the board and give it to the teacher. Upon exchange, the student should be given immediate access to the main reinforcer.

5

Discrete-trial teaching

In the next three chapters, we will continue to focus on the 'how' of teaching early numeracy to children with developmental disabilities. Although we will provide plenty of examples, our emphasis will be on explaining basic principles and guidelines so that you can adapt them to your own unique needs. In this chapter and in Chapter 6, we will explain three key instructional methods that teachers should use: discrete-trial teaching (this chapter), prompting and prompt fading, and error correction (Chapter 6). In Chapter 7 we will provide information on some additional teaching supports that can be used to maximize learning. There, we will focus on how teachers can help promote children acquiring skills that will be maintained and generalized.

Although the teaching practices may seem quite abstract as you read about them for the first time, when you begin to teach the student using these methods and acquire first-hand practical experience of them, you soon realize that they will help you teach mathematics to the student more effectively. Although the teaching may feel unnatural and awkward at the beginning, over time, as you observe how well the students are learning with this approach, you will gradually feel more at ease.

Learning to teach the student in the most effective way possible is like becoming skillful at any other difficult task. First of all, you need to learn the basics but then you need to follow through with extensive practice. In this chapter, we will teach you the basics, but it is only with practice that you will become more skillful in your abilities and more confident at using these techniques.

Discrete-trial teaching (DTT) forms the basis of the teaching programs presented in this book. In the first part of this chapter, we will provide a summary of discrete-trial teaching that will include the following components:

- A short overview describing salient features of the practice, including what it is, who it can be used with, and what skills it can be used to teach

- A description of the components of a discrete trial
- Guidance on how to deliver discrete-trial teaching effectively

What is discrete-trial teaching?

Discrete-trial teaching refers to a way of working with a student to teach new skills in a learning environment that is highly structured. Although it is described in this book as a method for teaching mathematical skills, it can be used to teach a variety of new skills in home, school, or community settings. Because discrete trials are often carried out in an intensive and repetitive fashion, quiet teaching areas with limited distractions are frequently used. Discrete-trial teaching can be used to teach students of all ability levels from early childhood through to adulthood. However, there is more evidence for using discrete-trial teaching with younger children who have a developmental disability, i.e., from 2 to 11 years of age (e.g., Smith, 2001).

Discrete-trial teaching is a method of teaching in very simple steps. Instead of teaching an entire skill in one go, each skill is broken down and 'built up' using discrete trials that teach one subskill at a time until mastery. It can be helpful initially to think of discrete-trial teaching as a series of teaching attempts, with each attempt or trial having a distinct beginning and end; hence the term 'discrete' trial. Within discrete-trial teaching, the use of antecedents and consequences is carefully planned and implemented. Positive praise and/or tangible rewards are used to reinforce the desired skills.

In discrete-trial teaching, using a one-to-one teacher:student teaching ratio, teaching begins with the teacher presenting a specific cue or instruction to the student, if necessary prompting the student's answer, and finally rewarding the student for their answer. For example, when teaching the student to be able to identify numerals, the student might be shown three numeral cards on the table, asked to 'Show me 7', prompted to touch the numeral 7, and rewarded with a tickle, praise, a small sweet or a chance to play with a favorite toy. This single cycle of instruction (antecedent–behavior–consequence) is known as a discrete trial.

Discrete trials may continue in this way for a short teaching session (lasting perhaps two to three minutes at a time), with there being anywhere between 8 and 12 discrete trials in a minute. After this brief teaching session, the student is usually offered a short break of a few minutes to play with a favorite toy or engage in some other preferred activity. Thus, in a three-minute teaching period a student may have been presented with around 30 learning opportunities and make around 30 responses. This is far more than in most traditional teaching approaches. Discrete-trial teaching also contrasts with traditional teaching methods in another way. In discrete-trial teaching, a very small amount of information is presented and the student's response is immediately sought. Thus, the student must be active and engaged in learning. This differs from other teaching approaches where large amounts of information are presented with no clearly defined target response on the student's part.

In discrete-trial teaching, each part of a skill is mastered before a teacher presents additional information to be learnt. For a skill to be mastered, the student would need to consistently come up with the right answer, without help, for a predetermined mastery criterion (e.g., for 10 consecutive correct responses). Data collection is an important part of discrete-trial teaching and is used to support decision making by providing teachers with important information about students' progress, challenges, and when they have mastered a skill. If teachers do not collect these data, it can be very difficult for them to keep track and remember if a skill has been mastered from one session to the next and, subsequently, if they should be moving on to a new teaching target. Data collection and data-based decision making are described in more detail in Chapter 8.

Components of a discrete trial

There are three main components of a discrete trial, which correspond to the three-term contingency described in Chapter 4. There is an *antecedent* (an instruction or other cue), the student response or *behavior*, and then an event that happens after the response – this is the *consequence* or feedback. Figure 5.1 is an example of these three main components of a discrete trial.

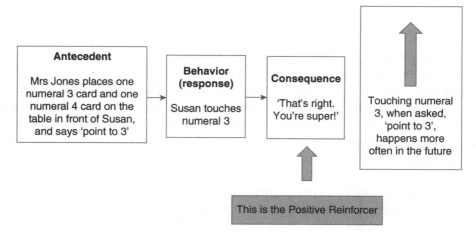

Figure 5.1 A discrete trial for a correct response

The antecedent

Each trial must have a clear beginning point. The first part of the discrete trial is often called an antecedent. Antecedents that affect behavior can come in a variety of forms. An antecedent to a target behavior (response) is often someone else's behavior, such as a teacher asking Monty, 'What number comes after 7?' This verbal instruction can be considered to be a type of antecedent that 'sets up' or 'cues' a response. Without the antecedent, Monty would not be able to provide a correct response. An antecedent does not always have to be a verbal instruction. It can be some other discrete event or visual cue, such as a teacher laying out on the table in front of the child, from left to right, numeral cards (e.g., 5, 4, 1, 3, 2). The presence of the array of cards may function as an antecedent that signals to the student that they should rearrange the cards in the correct order. Often, an antecedent involves both a verbal instruction and a visual stimulus (cue). In the example in Figure 5.1, the antecedent was the teacher (Mrs Jones) putting the numeral cards out on the table (the visual stimulus) and saying, 'Point to 3' (the verbal instruction). As both the numeral cards and Mrs Jones's instruction are needed for Susan to be able to respond correctly, both would be described as the antecedent.

Regardless of the form of the antecedent (visual, verbal instruction, etc.), the instructional component of a discrete trial is known as the discriminative stimulus (usually abbreviated to SD). As the student becomes more used to the teaching process, they will quickly learn that when an instruction (SD) is presented, a reward (positive reinforcement) will be provided for responding correctly to the instruction. The discriminative stimulus is a signal that reinforcement is available provided that the student responds correctly. The terms instruction, antecedent and discriminative stimulus (SD) are used interchangeably throughout this book to indicate the first component of a discrete trial.

The response

The next part of the discrete trial is called the behavior or response. This always comes after both the antecedent and a prompt (if there is one; see 'Prompt' section below). The student's behavior that is cued by the SD is called the response. In any discrete-trial procedure, the expected response should always be clear in advance and very carefully described. 'The student will select the numeral 3 from an array of three cards' and 'the student will count six dots forwards and backwards' are examples of clearly described expected responses, whereas suggesting that 'the student should give the correct answer' is not a clear definition of what would constitute a correct response. This level of specification helps to ensure that whoever is teaching the student is very clear about what level of response from the student should be reinforced. This idea will be described in more detail in the 'How do I deliver discrete-trial teaching effectively?' section below.

The consequence

The next part of the discrete trial is the consequence. Correct responses receive positive reinforcement (see Chapter 4), which may be in the form of verbal praise and/or through a token economy or delivery of other tangible reinforcers like small toys to play with or sweets. Figure 5.1 illustrates a discrete trial for when a student gives a correct response. The frequency with which Susan remembers to touch the numeral card 3 when she is asked depends on the consequence that happens right after she touches the card. If Susan likes being told, 'That's right. You're super' after she has touched the correct numeral card, her response has probably been reinforced and she will be a bit more likely in the future to touch the correct card when she is asked so that her teacher praises her again.

So far we have described the consequence a student may receive after they have given a correct response. Teachers also need to know what sort of a consequence to provide after a student has made a mistake. There are several types of error correction procedures that can be used, which are described in more detail in Chapter 6. The most important guideline to follow is that teachers should be careful about not providing any reinforcement for incorrect responses. This may appear to be self-evident, but plenty of teachers say something like, 'oh, that's a good try' in a very positive tone of voice or using the same tone that they would use for correct responses. This can be confusing for many students, particularly those with a language delay, who may struggle to understand the meaning of the individual words. They may also infer from the tone of your voice that they have done something right. Instead, you should try to give very clear feedback for incorrect responses, using a neutral voice, perhaps saying a phrase like 'let's try another one' or 'let's try that again'.

Additional component – the prompt

Often, the intended antecedent is not sufficient or strong enough to consistently lead to a correct answer, especially in early discrete trials in a phase of learning. In these situations, there may need to be a fourth component to discrete-trial teaching: the prompt. These additional hints or cues may be needed to get the ball rolling when children forget what they need to do. Prompts are usually presented at the same time as, or immediately after, an antecedent (i.e., within one second of the instruction). If it does not occur in this time frame, the instruction and the response may not occur closely enough in time for the student to understand that they are related. This sequence is illustrated in Figure 5.2.

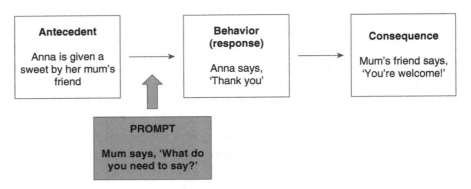

Figure 5.2   Everyday illustration of a prompt immediately following an antecedent

Figure 5.3 depicts a mathematical example for using a prompt. When Stephanie forgets what number comes after five, her teacher (Mr Brown) might give her the hint that the number that comes after five begins with the sound 'S'. This is called a partial verbal prompt or a partial phonemic prompt. There are many different types of prompts that can be used and are described in more detail in Chapter 6. One way of thinking of these prompts is as additional artificial antecedents that are temporary hints or clues that over time can be faded or reduced, and eventually eliminated altogether. This is absolutely crucial to avoid a student becoming what is called prompt dependent. If a student is to become fluent and confident with their responding, using prompting and prompt fading strategies is one way to achieve this (see fading prompts section, in Chapter 6). Chapter 6 will also describe those situations when a prompt should always be given or when a prompt should only be used under certain conditions.

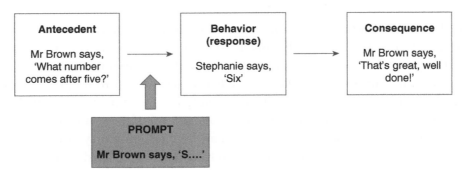

Figure 5.3   Example of a partial verbal prompt

How do I deliver discrete-trial teaching effectively?

The research literature on discrete-trial teaching has highlighted a number of recommendations for teachers regarding how to deliver discrete-trial teaching in the most effective way possible. Table 5.1 summarizes some key points to remember when delivering the antecedent.

Table 5.1   Guidelines for delivering the antecedent

1.	Prior to delivering the antecedent, gain the student's attention
2.	Use simple, clear instructions during the early stages of teaching:

  - Instructions should be simple and concise
  - Use the same word or phrase consistently
  - Present instructions using clear articulation

Guidelines for delivering the antecedent

Prior to delivering the antecedent, gain the student's attention

It is important to only deliver the antecedent when you can see that you have the student's full attention. If they are looking elsewhere, or doing something else, it is unlikely that they will be able to concentrate fully on what you are saying or doing. If they are not attending, this will reduce the likelihood that they will provide a correct answer that can be reinforced. Optimal learning, therefore, occurs when the student is paying attention. In fact, this is so important that on every single lesson plan there is a reminder at the start of the teaching procedure description for teachers to obtain the student's attention. If the student routinely exhibits poor attending, it is important that you try to teach them better attending skills so that they may gain maximal benefit from the numeracy program. Nine lesson plans for teaching attending and other 'learning to learn' skills can be downloaded from the website accompanying this book.

Use simple, clear instructions during the early stages of teaching

The student you are planning to work with will likely have encountered a multitude of mathematical instructions in school, both explicit and implicit, but will possibly have failed to understand what many of these instructions actually mean. It is your task to explicitly teach the student to understand and follow mathematical instructions. To facilitate the student's early learning (i.e., when you are just starting out trying to teach them a new skill), or if the student is struggling to learn a particular skill and has been for a while, it is best to simplify each instruction that is presented to them. This simplification can be achieved in one of three ways.

Instructions should be simple and concise

First, your instructions should be worded as simply and concisely as possible. This can help the student by highlighting the relevant part of the instruction to which they should be attending. For example, presenting the instruction, 'Can you tell me which card has the number 9 on, please?' may be difficult to understand because it contains too much extraneous information. Students may struggle to attend and retain the information from this wordy instruction, or find it difficult to pick out the salient piece of information to which they should be attending (e.g., the number 9). The simple instruction, 'Touch 9', may be much more accessible. A common mistake by teachers is that they wrongly presume that the student already has the prerequisite skill of being able to attend to and understand (discriminate) which part of a complex instruction contains the relevant cues. Unfortunately, many students do not have this skill already, and their learning in mathematics and in other areas is often impeded as a result.

That is not to say that as the student progresses and they master (i.e., learn) a particular skill, teachers should keep using these short instructions. As students get more adept at using their skills, teachers should aim to use more natural language akin to the language the students would hear in everyday situations away from structured teaching. This often means that the instructions should gradually become more complex and may have more words in them. This helps to promote generalization (i.e., the transference of learnt skills from a structured teaching situation to everyday situations) and may better prepare the student to be able to learn new skills more incidentally in natural situations. This idea will be discussed in more detail in Chapter 7, which provides more information on generalization.

Use the same word or phrase consistently

The second way to achieve simplification with an instruction is to decide on the exact wording of the instruction, and use the same word or phrase consistently. Consistency in instructions helps to minimize the student's confusion and maximize their learning. We may intend 'Put the numbers in order', 'Sequence these numbers for me', 'Arrange these numbers in the right way' to require the same response from the child. However, for a student with a developmental disability who may just be starting out on learning this new skill and who may also have language difficulties, each of these variations in the wording of the instruction may be perceived by them as having a different meaning (and so requiring a different, rather than the same, response each time). Varying instructions should be taught later, and not when you are starting to teach a skill. Being able to vary your instructions is called stimulus generalization. How you can best achieve this will also be covered in Chapter 7.

In the lesson plans, which can be downloaded from the website accompanying this book, we have sometimes specified a simple and concise verbal instruction in the teaching procedure section that teachers can use consistently during the early stages of teaching.

For example, in lesson plan A2.5 (Numeral Identification), the antecedent is clearly described as:

- Place numeral cards 1-3 on the table in front of the student in no particular order or position. Point to the card for 3 (visual antecedent)
- Say, 'What number (is this)?' (verbal instruction)

Sometimes, if it was felt important to convey the essence of the original instruction from the green book, recommendations for changing the wording are provided only in the 'help that may be provided' section of the lesson plan and not in the main teaching procedure section. Teachers should be responsive to their student's mastery of skills, and be prepared to use more natural language (that may be more varied and wordy) as soon as their student demonstrates that they are ready.

Present instructions using clear articulation

The third tool in simplifying instructions and making them as easy as possible to follow is that teachers should always present each instruction in a loud and confident voice, with clear diction differentiating one word from another.

Guidelines for the response

The research literature on discrete-trial teaching has also highlighted a number of guidelines for teachers regarding the child's response. These are summarized in Table 5.2.

Table 5.2 Guidelines for the response

1.	Know what quality of response is expected
2.	Reinforce responses only if they are completely free of unsuitable behaviors
3.	Give a maximum of three seconds to respond
4.	Reinforce the desired spontaneous responses
5.	Do not accept the student anticipating the response

Know what quality of response is expected

It is important that everyone who works with a student agrees upon, and is consistent with the definition of, the expected response from the student. This is especially important when the student is initially being taught a new skill. A clearly defined expected response can help to increase the objectivity of the teacher as it is clear to them what constitutes a correct response, and what needs to be reinforced. If there is more than one teacher working with a student, a clearly defined response can also help to promote a consistency of teaching between them. If one teacher is requiring that Callum touches each object slowly and deliberately at the same time as saying the corresponding number (at a rate of about one count per second) before delivering reinforcement, and another teacher is happy for Callum to quickly say, '1, 2, 3, 4, 5', barely touching the objects as he goes along the line, then this may be confusing for him. It will not be clear what he needs to do to earn reinforcement and subsequently what response he needs to repeat in the future to demonstrate the skill.

Here is another example of inconsistency between teachers that we sometimes encounter. For Copying and Saying Short Backward Number Word Sequences (see lesson plan A1.2), a teacher may deliver the instruction, 'Count backwards from 5 to 1'. If the response is not clearly defined beforehand, some teachers may hesitate and reinforce the student for saying '4-3-2-1', while other teachers or paraprofessionals working with the student require that the student says '5-4-3-2-1' before delivering any reinforcement. Again, this can be very confusing (and frustrating!) for the student, who will not be sure which answer they need to give subsequently. This can be a hindrance to their speed of acquisition of new skills.

The student then needs to have very clear messages about exactly what they need to do to earn reinforcement. If teachers change their expectations from one response requirement to another, this will reduce the effectiveness of the reinforcer. Having a clear definition of the response will allow for consistent delivery of reinforcement. The student's response should be reinforced only when their response matches the agreed upon definition of correct responding. In addition, if teachers are not consistent with their response requirements, they may end up trying to teach more than one response at a time for any particular skill. This is far too complex for many students with a developmental disability to be able to cope with in the early stages of implementing this teaching approach, and can understandably cause frustration on their part as they struggle to understand and keep up with what is expected of them.

To help teachers know the quality of the expected responses, all of the lesson plans provide a suggestion for a definition of the response for each skill to be taught. It is recommended that all teachers who may be working with a student follow this response requirement consistently, especially when they first start teaching a new skill. For example, for counting three objects with one-to-one correspondence (see lesson plan A3.1: Counting Items in One Collection), the criterion for correct responding is stated as being that the student should start to count within three seconds of hearing the instruction ('count how many') and that they should touch one object and say the number words at a rate of about one per second. This response should be consistently reinforced by all teachers. No one teacher should be able to decide to change these requirements during a teaching session, such as the student having to count to 10 to receive reinforcement or count at a much faster pace.

Occasionally, a response requirement may need to be individualized and adjusted from that recommended in the lesson plan. For example, a student with fine motor difficulties may find it difficult to manipulate their fingers correctly to be able to count using their fingers in order to keep track of the number of claps that somebody makes (see lesson plan A5.6: Using Fingers to Keep Track of Temporal Sequences of Movements). Their expected response, therefore, could be changed so that they carefully place each finger in turn on the table as they count (similar to playing sequential keys on the piano) as this may be easier for them to do. It is also important to note that the quality of the expected response can change over time based on the student's performance. For example, when teaching the skill of counting objects it may be beneficial at the beginning to slow down the speed with which a student is expected to touch an object and count out loud. As the student becomes more proficient, it is of course perfectly acceptable for a student to count and touch at a much faster pace, and indeed this would be a much more natural response and one which you might expect to see with children in typical environments who are proficient in this skill.

Although it is permissible for teachers to alter response requirements from that written in the lesson plan (e.g., to make responses easier or more challenging depending on individual requirements), it is crucial that any new requirements are agreed upon in advance with everyone working with the student, and then written down clearly for everyone to follow.

Reinforce responses only if they are completely free of unsuitable behaviors

Sometimes, the student may give a correct mathematical response at the same time as doing something else that might be considered unsuitable or incongruous. Here are two examples:

- The student provides a correct response but does this at the same time as standing up and edging away from their table. If you provide reinforcement at this point, you would be likely to also reinforce the standing up and edging away from the table and would get more similar unhelpful responses in the future.
- The student responds to a question or an instruction by linking several responses together. For example, if a teacher holds up a numeral card 3 and asks, 'What number?' the student may respond by saying '2…5…3?' Here, it is almost as if the student is fishing for the correct response. If a student's response is reinforced for finally settling on the correct response after a few attempts, they may continue to use this unhelpful strategy.

If the student provides an extraneous unsuitable behavior at the same time as a correct response, you should provide the same consequence as if it was an incorrect response. Give a neutral response, 'Let's try that again', present the instruction a second time and prompt the correct response if necessary. This is described in more detail in the error correction section, in Chapter 6.

Give a maximum of three seconds to respond

Generally, after delivering an instruction, teachers should allow no more than three seconds for a student to respond. If the student is to make a connection (association) between an instruction and their response, these two events must occur almost simultaneously (or as close in time as possible). The longer the time interval between the instruction and response, the more likely it is that the student will not be able to make the correct association between the two. Further, it increases the likelihood that any other events that occur after the instruction and before the student's response may be inadvertently associated with the instruction.

If there is no response within three seconds, this inaction (i.e., a non-response) should be considered to be an error response and the correct error correction procedure should be followed. For example, if the student fails to respond, the teacher should immediately repeat the instruction a second time and simultaneously prompt the correct response (prompts, prompt fading and error correction procedures are described in Chapter 6).

Allowing up to three seconds for a response means that students with visual and auditory processing difficulties have a sufficient amount of time to be able to process the antecedent information. This recommendation may need to be individualized to the student to some extent. Some teachers prefer to deliver discrete trials at a very fast pace (i.e., only allowing a second or two for a response) as this can help to keep the student focused and attending. However, if teachers expect some students to respond too quickly, this can be aversive and confusing for them. Another drawback with very fast-paced teaching is that typical teaching does not occur at such a rapid pace and this may limit the opportunities for generalization. These issues are discussed in more detail in Chapter 7. Some students with auditory processing difficulties may benefit from being given up to five seconds to respond, but, for other students, if teachers allow too much time, this may result in the student's attention wandering and them becoming bored in their session.

Reinforce the desired spontaneous responses

Although the quality of the expected mathematical responses is described in the lesson plans, occasionally students will go above and beyond what they are expected to do and surprise us with unexpected outstanding behavior and performance. As these variations are unique to the individual, you will need to be ready to reinforce these responses accordingly. Here are three examples based on our work with students:

1. Magnus, who ordinarily has very poor eye contact, looks directly at you with a big smile, at the same time as saying the correct number word.

2. Celia, who does not usually sit and do mathematical tasks for more than one minute, has just worked with her teacher for three minutes and remained seated the whole time.

3. Barney, who is non-verbal, says the number word 'seven' when he is asked to touch '7'. This is his first word. He has not been heard to speak before.

For all of these exceptional responses, you should apply additional (known as differential) reinforcement so as not to miss the opportunity to strengthen the student's learning. If the student is working for tokens and has three tokens left to obtain, you may say something like, 'you know, that was so amazing, I am going to give you the rest of your tokens straight away!'

Do not accept the student anticipating the response

We often encounter situations where students anticipate the response that they need to give. They may start to respond before the teacher has even finished presenting the instruction. For example, teacher says, 'Count from 1 to…', student says, '1-2-3-4-5'; teacher asks, 'What number comes after…?', student says, '4'. If this starts to occur, then a number of different things may be happening:

1. The student might be distracted and not paying attention. Here, you would need to repeat the instruction a second time to see if their attending improves, and you might also need to rethink the reinforcement on offer. If it is not powerful enough, this might reduce the student's motivation to pay attention to what you are saying. If poor attending continues to be a problem, consider teaching the attending program which can be downloaded from the website accompanying this book.

2. You are being predictable. Consider if you are always delivering your instructions in the same order. This can be especially problematic if teachers are using a data sheet that lists from top-down the skills they need to be teaching in a session. Try to mix up the order of the instructions that you give so that the student cannot anticipate the pattern. For example, sometimes start your teaching session with teaching activities for key topic five, sometimes key topic three. Do not always start your session with key topic one and work sequentially through the key topics.

3. The student might be guessing. Try not to permit guessing, as the student might be lucky and give a correct response. Giving reinforcement for guessing will only promote more guessing in the future and generate more uncertainty.

Guidelines for delivering a consequence

This section provides some recommendations for delivering consequences effectively. Some of the ideas have been mentioned already in Chapter 4 but are repeated here for clarification in the context of talking about discrete-trial teaching. Although instructions (SDs) and responses are specified in all of the accompanying lesson plans, the consequences are not. It will become apparent from reading the section below that your consequences will need to be tailored to the student you are working with. There are simply too many possible variations to provide examples in each of the lesson plans. Table 5.3 provides a summary of the guidelines for delivering a consequence during discrete-trial teaching.

Table 5.3   Guidelines for delivering a consequence

I.	Provide an immediate consequence
2.	Always praise correct responses
3.	Feedback should be unambiguously positive or negative
4.	Provide the best reinforcement for the best responses (differential reinforcement)
5.	Reinforce frequently at the beginning, and gradually fade
6.	Vary reinforcers

Provide an immediate consequence

Once you have identified a reinforcer, it is important that a reinforcer is given *immediately* upon occurrence of a correct response. For example, if you have asked the student, 'What number comes after four?' and they have replied 'five', immediately present the reinforcer ideally within one second of the response. As mentioned previously, this increases the likelihood that the student will remember the correct response and repeat it subsequently. If you delay any longer then this runs the risk of an intervening response (such as sliding off the chair) inadvertently being reinforced and so strengthened.

When the student responds incorrectly, immediate negative feedback (e.g., a neutral tone of voice and the teacher saying, 'you need to try that again') and the absence of reinforcement convey to the student that they have given the wrong answer. This should decrease the likelihood that the student will repeat the incorrect response in the future. Error correction procedures are described in more detail in Chapter 6.

Always praise correct responses

Always pair effective reinforcers (such as access to toys, food) with social reinforcement. For example, smile and praise the student ('well done!', or 'super!') at the same time as giving them a chocolate button or at the same time as handing over a favorite toy to play with. If the student is not motivated by praise initially, this pairing process can help them to learn to value social praise. You may start your teaching with using just primary reinforcers, such as food and drink, but if you always remember to present a social reinforcer such as praise at the same time as delivering a primary reinforcer, then over time you should be able to fade the use of primary reinforcers until you are using only more naturally occurring social reinforcers.

Feedback should be unambiguously positive or negative

The meaning of the feedback you provide should be unambiguous. Ambiguous responses to correct responses may include saying in an unenthusiastic distracted way, 'well done', or responding to incorrect responses by giving a big smile, and saying in a very positive tone of voice 'that wasn't right'.

Provide the best reinforcement for the best responses (differential reinforcement)

It is important that teachers get into the habit of using differential reinforcement. This can provide more information to the student regarding the quality of their response and what they need to do in the future to receive the highest levels of reinforcement. Thus, the best responses should always result in the best reinforcers; whereas responses that require prompting or those responses that are of poorer quality should receive a moderate level of reinforcement. Incorrect responses, on the other hand, should receive no reinforcement at all, but just a mild neutral, 'let's try again'.

Reinforce frequently at the beginning, and gradually fade

Once learning starts to occur, reinforcement should be faded as soon as possible to approximate what the student is likely to encounter in natural environments. This will help to promote generalization (see Chapter 7). As learning progresses, the student should be exposed to:

1. A reduced frequency of reinforcement (i.e. they receive reinforcement less often)
2. A decreased intensity of reinforcement (e.g., they do not get such a loud cheer when they provide a correct response), and
3. Increased delays to reinforcement (e.g., they do not get five minutes on an iPad immediately that they get their 10th token, but have to wait until break time to be able to obtain this main reinforcer).

A student cannot go through life expecting a big whoop and a cheer every single time that they provide a correct response. However, this may very well be necessary in the beginning of teaching, especially for those students who have not yet developed any mathematical skills at all or who have very few skills at their disposal. Similarly, for those students that have a history of engaging in challenging behavior when a mathematical task is presented to them, it may be extremely important to ensure that a reinforcer follows all correct responses in the beginning.

As the student masters each skill, however, start to spread out the reinforcement over trials by only intermittently delivering a reinforcer (e.g., one token approximately every three or four correct responses) or intermittently delivering the most powerful reinforcers (e.g., the chance to play with the most preferred toy happens only after about every fifth correct response). You should use continuous reinforcement (one reinforcer for each response) to *teach* a *new* response (i.e., for skills that are on acquisition); whereas intermittent reinforcement is used to maintain responding to skills that have already been learnt. As you will see in Chapter 7, fading reinforcement so that it starts to occur at a rate more typical of natural environments is an important step towards the generalization of skills outside of structured teaching situations. Chapter 7 will describe in more detail how and when to fade out reinforcement.

Vary reinforcers

The strength of any given reinforcer varies with how much a student is exposed to a reinforcer. Fairly mediocre reinforcers may gain value if a student has not had those reinforcers for a while; whereas even the most powerful reinforcers can lose their value if the student is given them too often. It is important that you vary reinforcers frequently and do not use the same items or activities too often. For example, if you intend to use iPad time as a reinforcer during Imogen's mathematics class, you probably want to make sure that she has not had a chance to play on the iPad for a period of time. If Imogen has not had access to the iPad for a while, she is more likely to want to work for the iPad, and you will have established the iPad as a more powerful reinforcer in that situation. You need to be careful though. While depriving Imogen of the iPad for a while may help to increase the value of the iPad as a reinforcer, you do not want to create a situation where Imogen thinks she has to work too hard just to get a few minutes on the iPad. If the work is perceived as being too hard in relation to the amount of reinforcement, the student may decide that it is just not worth the effort. To use another example, if you wanted to use chocolate buttons as a reinforcer in the afternoon, but Henry has just had a big lunch, the buttons would be unlikely to function as a reinforcer in the afternoon if Henry is full up. You might want to just use edibles as a reinforcer in the morning before lunch.

You should try to vary the types of reinforcers that you use during teaching and provide only small amounts of each particular reinforcer. Once you have identified your reinforcers (see Chapter 4), you can vary them by, for example, giving a high-five for one correct response, giving the student a chocolate button on the next correct response, and a favorite toy to play with for another correct response. Similarly, you should not monotonously repeat the same praise comment (e.g., 'Good') after every correct response. Instead, give a big smile and enthusiastically deliver lots of different praise comments one after the other (e.g., 'That's fantastic', 'Well done', 'What a great answer!').

To try to avoid reducing the value of reinforcers, you should also try to limit the quantity of a particular reinforcer. For example, you could give the student one chip (or crisp) for a correct response rather than a handful of chips. Or they could watch a favorite YouTube clip for a few seconds rather than for several minutes. Some teachers like to facilitate the degree of desire for reinforcers by limiting their availability outside of the teaching sessions, or holding back certain reinforcers for the most difficult-to-teach skills. For example, in some schools that we have worked in, students are only allowed time on the iPad after numeracy teaching sessions and not at any other time during the school day. If the student is allowed access to an iPad at numerous other times then this may mean that the iPad will fail to motivate them during their teaching sessions.

6

Using prompts in teaching

Prompts are the hints or cues that you can present to a student that will help them on their way to giving a correct response. Without the use of prompts, a teacher may never obtain the opportunity to reinforce and strengthen new skills. Prompts are used all the time in everyday life. When teaching a child to ride a bicycle for the very first time, a parent provides a maximum-strength prompt by holding onto both the child *and* the bicycle as they walk alongside, ensuring that the child does not fall off. Every effort that the child makes is praised (reinforced) by the parent telling them what a great job they are doing and how brave they are. Over time, as the parent starts to get the sense that their child is becoming more competent at balancing themselves on the bicycle, the parent starts to provide less physical assistance, perhaps by steadying the bicycle with just one hand rather than two, then gradually reducing the assistance even further, by releasing the remaining hand for a second or two as they run alongside the bicycle, just in case the child starts to wobble. Finally, the child is able to ride without any help at all.

In teaching early numeracy to children with developmental disabilities, you may start with a full complement of prompts, and provide highly powerful and potent reinforcement for the first independent responses. As the student becomes more adept at demonstrating the target skill, you may be able to gradually reduce the amount of assistance you provide as well as the intensity of the reinforcement on offer. The students who make the greatest gains are those whose teachers know how to use prompting, prompt fading, and error correction procedures properly. To be an effective teacher, it helps to understand that there are different types of prompts and prompt fading techniques. In addition, we naturally use prompts to facilitate learning in all sorts of situations. Distinguishing between different types of prompts, and then how to best use them, can enhance the effectiveness of teaching.

Prompt types

A wide range of prompts are suitable to use for the teaching of the mathematical skills described in this book.

Physical prompts

In physical or manual prompting, the teacher helps the student give the correct response by providing the student with manual help. This is sometimes called a *hand-over-hand* prompt. That is, the teacher guides the student's body through the motions that they need to do to give the correct response. A *full physical prompt* would involve taking the student's hand or body and moving it for them, so that they correctly respond to whichever direction has been given. For example, if you were to ask the student to 'make four claps' (lesson plan A6.3: Copying and Counting Monotonic Sequences of Sounds), you would place your hands over the student's hands and guide them to clap four times. Teachers often use physical prompts to help a student learn new skills outside of the mathematical domain. For example, when teaching children to write for the first time a teacher may place their hand over the child's hand to guide their movement when writing their letters. The use of full physical prompts should be faded as soon as possible, as they ought to be used only when there is no other option to get a student started on learning.

A *partial physical prompt* is similar. Here, you would still be touching the student, but your help is reduced somewhat so that you would only be gently guiding the student toward completing the response. In the previous example, the teacher might ask the student to 'make four claps' and gently nudge the student's wrists upwards to guide them towards the correct response. The student is then able to complete the response by clapping their hands the correct number of times. To use another example, a teacher may ask a student to 'make four claps' and then place their own hands either side of the student's closed hands on the fourth clap to prompt the student to stop clapping after the fourth clap.

Modeling prompts

When using *a modeling prompt,* a teacher would provide a visual demonstration of what the response looks like, by showing the student exactly what they need to do to respond or perform the task correctly. For example, if you asked the student to 'Put three blocks in the bucket' (see generalization suggestion, from lesson plan A3.2: Establishing a Collection of Given Numerosity), you would show them first what they need to do. If the prompt was successful, they would copy the action you have just shown them.

Modeling is routinely used by teachers working with all students. For students with a developmental disability, many of the skills you will want to teach will be complex for them and modeling may be an effective way to help teach these skills. To be able to use modeling as a prompt, the student would first of all need to be able to imitate an adult's actions. Teachers should not presume that students with a developmental disability already have this skill. Many students will need to be first taught how to imitate before modeling prompts can be used. It is well worth persevering with teaching this skill, as there are advantages to using modeling as a prompt. First, many of the responses you will want the child to learn are complex and are not easily taught without modeling. Second, in the early stages of teaching the teacher will model the correct responses. Ultimately, other people (adults, and peers) may act as models and offer the child additional learning opportunities through *observational learning*. This is when learning occurs simply through observing the behaviors of others and watching what they do. In observational learning, seemingly no reinforcement is needed for demonstration of a skill or at least nothing as obvious and contrived as with discrete-trial teaching. This is the goal for teachers: that a student can learn skills through observation alone and without needing to be formally taught or relying on extrinsic reinforcement. If a student is able to learn some skills observationally, this can free up valuable teaching time for the instruction of other, more complex skills that do need to be directly taught. Four lesson plans for teaching the important prerequisite skill of motor imitation can be downloaded from the website accompanying this book.

As with physical prompts, modeling prompts can be faded to *partial modeling prompts* where a teacher provides only a partial demonstration of the expected response. If a student has been asked to 'Make a finger pattern of three' (lesson plan A5.3: Simultaneous Patterns for 1 to 5, fingers seen) and the teacher begins by giving a complete model of the skill on the first trial, they may fade their modeling prompt on the next trial by waiting to see if the student raises their thumb and first finger without help and only then demonstrating the correct pattern with the addition of the third finger. This is an example of the full modeling prompt on the first trial being faded to a partial modeling prompt on the second. See also the fading prompts section below.

Gestural prompts

Gestural prompts are gestures or non-verbal actions that the student can watch that give them some indication as to what they should do. Pointing or nodding are two examples of gestural prompts. For example, if you were to ask a student to 'give me the card with five dots' (see generalization suggestion, lesson plan A4.1: Ascribing Numerosity to Patterns and Random Arrays), and they had not selected the correct card within three seconds, you might prompt by repeating the request at the same time as pointing to the five-dot pattern. To give another example, you may ask a student to put five numeral cards in the correct sequence (lesson plan A2.3: Sequencing Numerals). They may quickly and assuredly sequence the first three numeral cards, but then their hand hovers over numeral card 4 and they look at you for confirmation that they have chosen the correct card to sequence next. If you nod in affirmation at that point, this would be an example of a gestural prompt. Pointing at, gesturing toward, or glancing at the correct item are sometimes referred to collectively as non-specific prompts. Generally, they are used to assist a student in teaching programs when they are required to select the correct object or picture from an array of items.

Although gestural prompts can be carefully planned and subsequently teachers need to know to fade them eventually, there is a danger in using inadvertent gestural prompts. Inadvertent prompting is when you provide assistance of which you are not aware. For the numeral recognition program where a student is required to select a named numeral card (e.g., lesson plan A2.4), an inadvertent prompt might include glancing toward the numeral card you would like a student to select, or smiling as their hand moves toward the correct card. For the numeral identification program where the student is required to name a numeral card that they can see (e.g., lesson plan A2.5), an example of inadvertent prompting may include mouthing the number word you want the student to say as you focus on the task. If the student is learning a new skill at a much faster rate than they would usually do, this may be a sign that you are using accidental prompts. Another clue may be that the student is strong with demonstrating a particular skill with one teacher but is struggling with demonstrating the skill with another. This may be an indication that one teacher is using inadvertent prompts whereas the other is not. You can test out potential problems by concentrating on making sure that you remove all glances, facial expressions and other gestures when you deliver an instruction. If the student 'suddenly' cannot do the task anymore, this is probably because you were prompting the task all along.

Verbal prompts

A *verbal prompt* can be considered to be a type of modeling where a teacher demonstrates the verbal response that a student is required to say. A full verbal prompt is when a teacher verbalizes the entire phrase or word that is needed for a correct response. For example, if you are teaching a student to identify numerals (e.g., lesson plan A2.5), you might give the instruction, 'What number is this?' while holding up the numeral card 3 and giving the verbal prompt, 'Say three'. A partial verbal prompt might be to fade back, 'Say, three' to 'three', and then to fade back further to 'th…'.

Just as modeling action prompts can be ineffective for those children who do not have the prerequisite skill of being able to imitate another person's actions, verbal prompts also cannot be used successfully with children with severe language delays who find it difficult to correctly imitate (echo) sounds and words that are modeled to them (e.g., if a teacher says, 'Say, cup', being able to repeat 'cup'). Five lesson plans for teaching the important prerequisite skill of verbal imitation can be downloaded from the website accompanying this book.

Visual prompts

Visual prompts can be pictures, text, photos and even videos. An example of a visual prompt is when the teacher says, 'touch 2' (see lesson plan A2.4: Numeral Recognition), at the same time as holding up a numeral card 2. This helps the student to *match-to-sample*. Matching to sample involves identifying from an array of numeral cards the one that 'matches' the sample numeral card that the teacher is holding. Another example of a visual prompt provided by the teacher is that the teacher says, 'count up to 8', at the same time as holding up a numeral 8 card. This helps the student to know at which point they need to stop counting. Five lesson plans for teaching prerequisite matching skills can be downloaded from the website accompanying this book.

Textual prompts are also a type of visual prompt that can be used with students who are able to read. They are written cues for responding, which can be very helpful when verbal instructions can be too much to comprehend by themselves. One difficulty with relying on verbal instructions alone is that they are transient. Once spoken, the words disappear. Some students with a developmental disability find it difficult to quickly work out what spoken instructions mean, and then remember what has been said once the words have been spoken. Textual prompts provide a visual means to help a student understand and remember what is required of them in addition to the verbal instruction. For example, to teach the student to 'make four claps' (see lesson plan A6.3: Copying and Counting Monotonic Sequences of Sounds), you might write down the instruction on a card and then show them this written cue at the same time as verbalizing the instruction. The student can then keep referring to the textual prompt after you have spoken to remind them how many times they need to clap.

> ## Make four claps

Positional prompts are also a type of visual prompt. These can be used in any program where the student is required to select an item from a display of items, but the teacher positions the target item closer to the student. For example, for the numeral recognition program where a student is required to select a named numeral card (e.g., lesson plan A2.4), when teaching a student to select the numeral '3' from a display of numeral cards (3, 5, 6, 7), the teacher may place the numeral 3 card close to the student and the other numeral cards further away (see Figure 6.1).

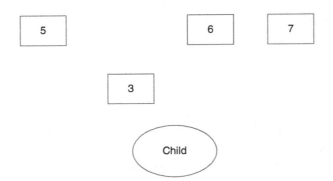

Figure 6.1 Example of a positional prompt for teaching numeral recognition (lesson plan A2.4)

When the instruction ('touch 3') is given, the close proximity of the numeral 3 card can facilitate correct responding. Over a number of trials, the numeral 3 might gradually be moved further back until it is in the same line as the other cards (so no positional prompt is provided). Teachers sometimes use inadvertent positional prompts where they unwittingly place the item to be selected closer to the student, so it is important to check that you are not doing this.

Deciding which prompt to use

There are a number of different types of prompts that can be used in different teaching situations. Some prompts may be more effective than others for particular teaching targets, and some prompts may be more effective for one student compared to another (see Leaf et al., 2016). Prompting strategies may need to be individualized to both the task and the student. Physical and gestural prompts are most suited to learning tasks that have a motor component (e.g., making temporal patterns and temporal sequences of movements – see lesson plans A6.1–A6.4; or selecting named numeral cards through touching – see lesson plan A2.4). Verbal prompts are most suited to those tasks that require a verbal response of some kind.

Conducting an informal assessment of prerequisite skills for using the different prompt types might also be beneficial. For example, as mentioned previously, to be able to use modeling as a prompt, the student would first of all need to be able to imitate an adult's actions. To assess whether the student would be able to respond to a model prompt, you could lay out different objects on the table with which the student is not familiar (e.g., hole puncher, stapler and ruler), deliver the instruction (e.g., 'touch the stapler'), and then touch the target item. You would then wait to see if the student is able to respond correctly to that prompt type. Similarly, to assess if a student is able to follow a gestural prompt, you could deliver a similar instruction but for a different item (e.g., 'touch the hole puncher'), point toward the correct item and then wait to see if the student follows the pointing prompt. If the student is able to follow these prompts during the test, you can probably use them during your teaching.

The student's preferences may be particularly important when deciding which prompt to use, especially as some students with a developmental disability may find physical contact aversive. As an example, Magnus's teacher knows that he does not like to be touched lightly on the arm because this results in him pulling away. She knows that he responds very well to modeling prompts and he can imitate movements and verbal responses. She decides subsequently to use verbal, gestural and modeling prompts during teaching but to not use any physical prompts.

Fading prompts

The main advantage of using prompts is that they help a desired response to occur, so that the response can subsequently be reinforced and strengthened, and the student can progress with learning a new skill. The main disadvantage of using prompts is that when the student is provided with a prompt, they are not responding correctly by themselves. Instead, responding to the prompt is being reinforced. This can become a serious problem. Some children may become reliant on the prompt for responding correctly and may become prompt dependent.

To avoid *prompt dependence*, once the student is responding easily to prompts and appears to be beginning to understand the task, you should aim to use the least intensive prompt that you can or no prompt at all (while still allowing the student to be successful). You may start with intensive assistance, but then gradually and systematically reduce the intensity of the prompt until the student can correctly respond on their own (i.e., without the prompt). This process is called *prompt fading*. It is more straightforward to choose one type of prompt for teaching a particular skill (physical, gestural, verbal, etc.) and then to fade the intensity of the prompt within that prompt type, rather than to move across different prompts during the teaching of one skill. There are several strategies that can be used for ensuring that you are not encouraging prompt dependence. We will describe three of the best-known ones:

- Least-to-most prompting
- Most-to-least prompting
- Using a time delay

Least-to-most prompting

Here, teachers start with the least intensive prompt first to see if that works. If it does not, they systematically provide more help. For example, if you ask a student 'what number?' when you hold up numeral card 3 and she does not respond, you might then give a partial verbal prompt ('th…'). If she does not say three at that point, you might then give her more of the verbal prompt ('thr…'). If that still is not successful at eliciting the response, you might then provide a full verbal prompt ('three') to say the number word three in the presence of the card.

One of the main advantages in using least-to-most prompts where you develop a prompt hierarchy that progresses in intensity for a particular prompt type, is that it is the approach that teachers more instinctively use. We want the student to be as independent as possible, which means we intuitively try to provide the least amount of help possible. Another advantage of this approach is that it gives the student an opportunity at the beginning of each trial to be as independent as they can.

Most-to-least prompting

In most-to-least prompting, you start with the *most* intensive prompt within a particular prompt type and gradually reduce the intensiveness of the prompt, with the aim that you finish your teaching session with an independent unprompted response. Using an example of teaching a student to clap three times (see lesson plan A6.3: Copying and Counting Monotonic Sequences of Sounds), you might start your teaching on the first trial by giving her a full hand-over-hand prompt to clap the required number of times. This would then gradually be faded to the first partial physical prompt (lighter force; the physical prompt consists of nudging her wrists rather than her hands), and then faded further to the second partial physical prompt (a very light nudge) until finally she is responding independently. Most-to-least prompting is a way of fading prompts by reducing their intensity, like with lessening the amount of manual guidance that is provided in the example above, or with gradually reducing the volume of a verbal modeling prompt over successive trials.

One of the main advantages of using most-to-least prompting over least-to-most prompting is that most-to-least prompting typically reduces the number of errors that a student makes. Most-to-least prompting is often used with errorless teaching, described in the section below, as a way of ensuring the student is as successful as possible and makes as few errors as possible. A disadvantage of the approach is that it can take a long time to get the student to respond independently, as the teacher may be prompting too much in an effort to prevent any errors.

Another problem may occur when the child, to receive reinforcement, is inadvertently taught to pay attention to smaller and smaller elements of the prompt which might interfere with their attention to the initial instruction. One way of addressing this issue is to gradually withhold reinforcement for prompted trials while providing maximal reinforcement for unprompted trials (differential reinforcement). By reducing the intensity of the prompt while concurrently reinforcing the student's response to the instruction, the prompt becomes a less reliable cue for responding than the instruction. One popular way of fading prompts and shifting transfer of control from the prompt to the instruction is by doing what is called a transfer trial immediately after prompted trials. This procedure is described in more detail in the section below on error correction procedures.

Time delay procedures

Most-to-least prompting and least-to-most prompting can work very well for any tasks that require a physical action, but they can be more difficult to apply for some verbal tasks, such as Copying and Saying Short Forward Number Word Sequences (lesson plan A1.1) or saying what number word comes after a given number (lesson plan A1.6). As teachers cannot physically prompt a student to talk or physically prompt them to say the answer required, they are more limited in the types and number of prompts they can use. For example, if a teacher is providing a verbal model for a number word this can be more difficult to break down into substeps (other than the whole word vs. the first sound of the word, or saying the word more quietly over successive trials). Using time delay can overcome this difficulty. Time delay is a strategy that can work well for verbal prompts because you delay the delivery of the entire prompt and you do not have to rely on using more or less intrusive prompts (although you can combine the two strategies, as you will see).

Time delay is when you start with an immediate prompt right after providing the initial instruction. So, if I am teaching Arthur to say 'eight' when I show him the numeral card '8', I would show him the numeral card and then immediately I would say, 'say, 8'. If he echoes (imitates) my response, I would provide some form of reinforcement for following the verbal prompt such as a praise comment. When Arthur is reliably repeating or following the verbal prompt and giving the correct response, I would start to present the instruction and *wait* or withhold the prompt for a second or two to see if he can provide a correct response without the prompt. Such a trial is sometimes called a *probe trial*. An example of this time delay procedure is shown in Figure 6.2.

Student easily follows the verbal prompt and provides a correct response	Mrs Smith:	Holds up a numeral 8 card and says, **'What number? Eight'**
	Arthur:	'Eight'
	Mrs Smith:	'Great' (minimal reinforcement)
Time delay procedure	Mrs Smith:	Holds up a numeral 8 card and says, **'What number?'**
	Arthur:	NO RESPONSE
	Mrs Smith:	Waits three seconds
	Arthur:	'Eight'
	Mrs Smith:	'That's amazing. Well done', and hands over favorite toy (maximal reinforcement)

Figure 6.2 Time delay procedure when the student provides a correct response

This example illustrates that Arthur has learnt to repeat the response 'eight' and that he did not require further prompting. You will notice in the example, as is important with all prompt fading strategies, that Mrs Smith, the teacher provided a more powerful reinforcer when Arthur responded independently without the verbal prompt. More independence should always receive more reinforcement. Providing this differentiated reinforcement based on whether the student responded correctly with or without a prompt, or with a lesser degree of prompt, is a critical component of prompt fading and is critical to students' success.

If there is no response to a time delay prompt, you would need to use the level of prompt that you deem to be the most suitable for the student (e.g., by combining the time delay with most-to-least or least-to-most prompting). This is illustrated in Figure 6.3.

Student easily follows the verbal prompt and provides a correct response	Mrs Smith:	Holds up a numeral 8 card and says, **'What number? Eight'**
	Arthur:	'Eight'
	Mrs Smith:	'Great' (minimal reinforcement)
Time delay procedure	Mrs Smith:	Holds up a numeral 8 card and says, **'What number?'**
	Arthur:	NO RESPONSE
	Mrs Smith:	Waits three seconds
	Arthur:	NO RESPONSE (after 3 seconds)
	Mrs Smith:	**'ay…'** (having previously determined that least-to-most partial verbal prompts are usually effective with Arthur)
	Arthur:	**'Eight'** (if he had not responded with the correct response, at this point Mrs Smith would have used a more intrusive full verbal prompt, 'say, eight')

Figure 6.3 Time delay procedure when the student does not respond to the time delay prompt

In Chapter 5 and in this chapter, we have provided guidance on how to use prompting and prompt fading procedures correctly. Table 6.1 summarizes these guidelines.

Table 6.1 Key guidelines for using prompts effectively

1.	The prompt should occur at the same time as, or within one second of, the instruction
2.	Select a prompt that provides just enough help to ensure success but is never more than is needed
3.	If your first prompt does not work, move up a prompt hierarchy that progresses in intensity for a particular prompt type (least-to-most prompting)
4.	If you have prompted the student, and they follow the prompt, move quickly to the next trial and repeat the instruction either with no prompt (using time delay) or a lesser degree of prompt (most-to-least prompting)
5.	Use differential reinforcement for unprompted trials
6.	Be vigilant about avoiding inadvertent prompting

Libby et al. (2008) also provide some useful guidelines on how to decide what is the most effective prompting strategy to use:

- If you are only just starting work with a child, and you do not know how they best learn, most-to-least is likely the best default response prompting technique.
- Most-to-least is also more preferable if you know that errors can increase problem behavior. However, using most-to-least without a time delay may produce slower acquisition even though it minimizes errors.
- Least-to-most may be the preferred strategy for those children who have already shown that they can learn quickly with this prompting method.
- If you would like to compare the effectiveness of different prompting strategies, try to ensure that the tasks you choose are of equal difficulty and that the student has not had more exposure to one of the tasks than the other prior to the comparison.

It is also important that you learn to record data so that you can monitor a student's progress frequently. This will help to ensure that errors do not stall learning, and that you are fading prompts. Chapter 8 provides guidance on how to collect data and how to interpret the data effectively.

Error correction

Error correction is a technique for correcting errors that have not been prevented. In error correction, the question or direction is re-stated, a prompt is provided, then that prompt is immediately faded out using what is called a *transfer trial*. Providing consistent and well-considered error correction to incorrect responses is just as important as remembering to provide positive reinforcement for the correct responses. Four steps that are important to remember for error correction are summarized in Table 6.2.

Table 6.2   How to correct errors

1.	Do not provide reinforcement
2.	Re-state the question or direction, and prompt
3.	Fade prompt using a transfer trial
4.	Distract and retest to see if the student can remember

Do not provide reinforcement

In Chapter 5, we described how important it is that teachers should not provide any reinforcement for incorrect responses. Teachers should always try to give very clear feedback for incorrect responses using a neutral voice, perhaps saying a phrase like 'no, that's not right', or 'let's try that again'.

There is another way that a student's errors may be unwittingly reinforced. Let's take the example of 6-year-old Caitlin. She has autism, can make vocalizations and is considered by her teachers to be fairly numerate. When she is shown a domino card with six dots (see lesson plan A4.1: Ascribing Numerosity to Patterns and Random Arrays) and is asked 'how many dots?' she replies '1-2-3-4-5-6'. Although close, this is not the required response as the objective of this task is that the student is able to ascribe numerosity to patterns of dots on domino cards without counting the dots (similar to when we can immediately recognize and label patterns of dots on a rolled dice without counting each dot in turn). So the answer for Caitlin should be simply 'six' and nothing else. This is a frequent mistake made by students, who often presume that they need to count out the numbers in sequence until they reach the correct number. This is perhaps to be expected as there are many other counting targets, particularly in the Emergent Stage, where saying number word sequences is required.

Teachers are often not sure what to do here, as the student is *sort of* correct. Many teachers respond by reinforcing the counting response. A teacher who is not familiar with the proper error correction procedure might respond by saying something like, 'well, I suppose there are 1-2-3-4-5-6 dots, you're right there, it is six dots'. It is not that Caitlin has some cognitive difficulties that are preventing her from learning the correct response to 'how many dots?', it is just that these errors have been reinforced so many times that she thinks that is the correct way to answer.

Another common area of confusion for children is that they mistake the numeral 6 for the numeral 9, or the numeral 6 for the numeral 8. Again, the teacher may try to manipulate the correct answer from the incorrect answer, so if the teacher holds up '6' and Barnabas says 'eight', the teacher may respond by saying something like, 'well, I can see that it looks a little like an 8, you're right there, but it's a 6'. But since Barnabas did not say the word 'six' for himself, it is the word 'eight' that ends up being reinforced and strengthened.

Re-state the question or direction, and prompt

In Chapter 5 we emphasized that you should know the quality of the expected response and that this should be written clearly in the lesson plan for each skill to be taught. If the student deviates in any way from what is written in the lesson plan, they have made an error and you need to respond accordingly. Provide clear feedback in a neutral voice ('no, that's not right, let's try again') and then immediately re-state the question or direction and provide an appropriate prompt. This is sometimes called the no-prompt procedure because you are allowing the student to make a mistake (the 'no') and then responding to the mistake with a prompt on the second trial. Using the previous example, by prompting Barnabas to say 'six', by providing the partial verbal prompt, 's…'.

Fade prompt using a transfer trial

It is important that the teacher strives for an independent unprompted response so that the student does not become prompt dependent. The teacher should immediately ask the question again *without* a prompt. When the teacher asks the question for a second time immediately after the prompt (e.g., by saying, 'right, what number is it?'), this is called a transfer trial.

The aim of the transfer trial is to move Barnabas on from responding with the correct answer only when he receives the prompt to being able to provide a correct answer without the prompt. During the transfer trial, the teacher could either fade the prompt completely, perhaps by waiting a few seconds to see if Barnabas is able to say the word 'six' with no prompting at all (i.e., by using a time delay prompt fading procedure) or they could provide a lesser degree of prompt, such as the partial verbal prompt, 's…'.

	Mrs Brown:	Holds up a numeral 6 card and asks, **'What number?'**
	Barnabas:	'Eight'
Does not provide reinforcement	Mrs Brown:	'Let's try that again'
Re-states question and prompts		Puts the 6 card down for a brief moment to signal the end of the trial, and then re-presents the card and repeats the question, **'What number?'** and immediately prompts the answer, **'Six'**
	Barnabas:	'Six'
Transfer trial	Mrs Brown:	'Right'. Puts the 6 card down briefly and then re-presents the card and repeats the question. **'What number?'** (fading prompt).
	Barnabas:	'Six' (with no prompt)
	Mrs Brown:	'That's super, well done' (and hands over preferred toy to play with)

Figure 6.4   Example of an error correction procedure with a transfer trial

You may have noticed from the example that, for incorrect responses, no reinforcement is given, even after the correction. Instead, there is a very brief acknowledgment that the student had responded (i.e., teacher saying 'right'). Remember what was said about differential reinforcement earlier? This is an important concept to consider for error correction too. You can provide some low-magnitude reinforcement, like a brief praise comment (e.g., 'good') for some children for correct responses that have followed a prompt, but try to remember to keep the highest preferred reinforcement for the *unprompted* correct responses, especially if you have been trying for quite a while to teach a particular skill. You do not want to teach the student that they can give an incorrect answer, that they can be helped by their teacher, and they still get the best reinforcer. Transfer trials are incredibly easy to use and can be an extremely effective method in helping students learn to be more independent with their responding.

Distract and retest to see if the student can remember

There is an additional step after the transfer trial which is also helpful. If you stop your teaching with the transfer trial, how can you be absolutely certain that the student has really learnt the skill and is not simply remembering to repeat what you have just said or modeled? You need to double-check that they can still remember what you have just shown them to do. Here, it is helpful to use what is sometimes called a *distractor trial*.

A distractor trial is when you ask the student to do something that is completely unrelated to the current task. Using the previous example, if you have been teaching Barnabas to label the numeral 6, and he has responded correctly after the transfer trial, you could then ask him to follow a simple instruction such as 'clap your hands' or 'touch your nose'. It needs to be something quick, but easy for the student. The important point is that you just want to distract them from what you have prompted for a brief moment. Immediately after you have presented the distractor trial, it is time to re-present the original instruction again. You are checking that the prompt you used the first time was successful and that it did help the student learn the skill. You may start with just presenting one distractor trial but then build up to having several distractor trials between the transfer trial and the re-presentation of the initial instruction. You would be checking for retention of the skill over an increasing amount of time. This sequence for correct responding is depicted in Figure 6.5. If the student gets the answer wrong at the end of the sequence (after the distractor trials), you start again at the beginning of the process.

	Mrs Brown:	Holds up a numeral 6 card and says, '**What number?**'
	Barnabas:	'Eight'
Does not provide reinforcement	Mrs Brown:	'Let's try that again'
Restates question and prompts		Puts the 6 card down for a brief moment to signal the end of the trial, and then re-presents the card and repeats the question, '**What number?**' and immediately prompts the answer, '**Six**'
	Barnabas:	'Six'
Transfer trial	Mrs Brown:	'Great'. Puts the 6 card down briefly and then re-presents the card and repeats the question. '**What number?**' (fading prompt).
	Barnabas:	'Six' (with no prompt)
	Mrs Brown:	'That's super' (and puts the 6 card down)
Distractor trials	Mrs Brown:	'Clap your hands'
	Barnabas:	Claps his hands
	Mrs Brown:	'Good, touch your nose'
	Barnabas:	Touches his nose
	Mrs Brown:	'Great, how old are you?'
	Barnabas:	'Nine'

(Continued)

Figure 6.5   (Continued)

Retest	Mrs Brown:	'Good', (holds up 6 numeral card) **'What number?'**
Independent response	Barnabas:	'Six'
	Mrs Brown:	'That is wonderful, well done' (and hands over preferred toy to play with)

Figure 6.5   Example of prompt, transfer trial, distract, and retest sequence

Errorless teaching

Prevention of errors can also be promoted with errorless teaching: arranging things in a learning program to maximize success. If you think that there is even a very small chance that the student is going to give the wrong answer or is not going to be able to follow an instruction, you could deliver a prompt simultaneously (at the same time) with delivering the instruction. For this reason, errorless teaching is sometimes called the simultaneous prompting or zero second prompting method. If you do this, you will ensure a correct response each time as you are not allowing the student an opportunity to make a mistake. For example, if you were asking a student to tell you the number of dots on a domino card (see lesson plan A4.1: Ascribing Numerosity to Patterns and Random Arrays), you would prompt them immediately (simultaneously) that you have delivered the instruction by providing either a full prompt, 'how many dots? Say three', or a partial verbal prompt, 'what number? Thr...' and the student says 'three'.

Another way that errorless teaching is used is to intervene with prompts when you see that a student is going to get the answer wrong if they continue. The prompt is then slowly faded to promote accuracy with the fewest errors (i.e., using most-to-least prompting). For example, if you are teaching a student to recognize numerals and you have asked them to 'touch number 5' from a selection of three cards on the table, and they reach their hand in the direction of the numeral 7, you could quickly guide their hand back toward the numeral 5 card before they have touched the numeral 7 card. Here, you would be interrupting their response and using a partial physical prompt *before* they have actually touched the incorrect numeral 7.

Intervening with prompts when you can see that the student is going to get the answer wrong can be helpful if you catch the potential error very early in a response. A disadvantage of this approach is that you run a great risk of building the error into the learning. For example, if the student goes to touch the wrong numeral card you might stop him midway and guide to the correct numeral. He then might always move his hand to hover over any numeral card when you say, 'touch...' with the expectation that you will guide him to the correct card.

As with the no-prompt procedure, when you are allowing the student to make a mistake (the 'no') and then responding to the mistake with a prompt on the second trial, if you are using errorless teaching it is crucial that you try to fade the prompts as soon as possible using the transfer trial procedures described above. This could either be through fading the intensity of the prompt on the transfer trial, or using a time delay prompt where you wait a few seconds to see if the student is able to respond independently.

The rationale for using errorless teaching is a simple one. People tend to enjoy their learning experiences more when they have a high success rate. In addition, if a student is practicing a new skill repeatedly (as is the case with discrete-trial teaching) in the hope that the skill will eventually be mastered, it could be beneficial to be practicing doing something right nearly all the time rather than practicing something over and over, only sometimes correctly (i.e., through trial and error learning). In deciding whether to use error correction or errorless teaching, you might want to consider the advantages and potential pitfalls of their use, which are summarized in Table 6.3.

Table 6.3   Advantages and potential pitfalls of error correction and errorless teaching

Error correction

Advantages	Potential pitfalls
Error correction parallels more typical teaching styles that allow errors, and then provides prompting as a correction procedure. This method comes more naturally to teachers. Children may come into contact frequently with error correction in other areas of their daily life.	Although some students are able to learn from their mistakes, many students, particularly those with a developmental disability, find it difficult to do this. Learning from mistakes requires a student to be able to problem solve what they did wrong. Although they can often learn that what they did was wrong, it can be difficult for them to work out what it is they should do next and how they can rectify their incorrect response.
For some children, it can be highly efficient as they are able to learn from their errors. They make a mistake a few times, get prompted, and then learn how to answer correctly without help.	Some children with a developmental disability do not respond well to being corrected, and this can create some behavioral difficulties.

(Continued)

Table 6.3   (Continued)

Errorless teaching

Advantages	Potential pitfalls
Prompting is paired with correct responding and more rapid reinforcement, so children can come into contact with reinforcement more frequently. If students are successful and learning is fun, prompting may be experienced as pleasant and positive. The opposite effect can occur when a student is prompted as part of a correction procedure, prompting may become aversive for some students. **Errorless teaching** can help improve motivation for learning for those students who are difficult to motivate, and this can improve their engagement.	If prompt fading techniques are not followed properly, the student can become prompt dependent. They learn to wait for the prompt.
Prompting ensures accuracy and a history of reinforcement for correct responding. This may in turn reduce errors.	Learning may take a long time for some students using errorless teaching, because it can take a long time to successfully fade out the prompts.

There are also some guidelines that might help you to decide between error correction and errorless teaching for an individual student, which are summarized in Table 6.4.

Table 6.4   Guidelines for deciding between errorless teaching and error correction

Errorless teaching	Error correction
May be right for the student if:	
They are beginning to learn a new skill for the first time	They appear to be able to learn from their errors
They have a history of struggling to learn a particular skill: they are making very little progress even after a long time	They can sit, attend, and learn without challenging behavior for at least 10-minute intervals
They have a history of inappropriate behavior to escape or avoid the learning environment	You have noticed that it is difficult to fade prompts when they are provided
They struggle with motivation to stay engaged during teaching sessions	

The learner is always right

In the last three chapters, we have introduced a lot of different ideas about how to deliver the best possible teaching of early numeracy to children with developmental disabilities. There is a saying in Applied Behavior Analysis that some of you may have heard already: 'the learner is always right' or 'the learner knows best'. If a student (learner) is not learning, then it is not their fault. Our students will tell us if what we are doing as teachers is working.

A common scenario is when a teacher has been trying to teach a skill for several weeks and the student is not mastering the skill. Teachers may say, 'he doesn't have the cognitive skills to learn' or 'she is not able enough to do this'. Provided that the student does have the prerequisite skills described earlier (see attending skills in Chapter 5, motor imitation, verbal imitation and matching skills in this chapter), the student *is* able enough and they should be able to learn mathematical skills using this program. It is not the student's fault (or their ability to learn) that is responsible for their failure to master skills. Rather, it is something about the teaching that is not working and the teacher is in the best position to change what they are doing. We are not blaming teachers here. There are very many pressures that affect a teacher's ability to deliver good teaching. However, as teachers, we are responsible for making necessary changes until the desired results are achieved and the student has learnt what we are teaching.

7

Ensuring learning lasts

Chapters 4–6 described how to teach children to learn mathematical skills during very structured teaching sessions. Most children can learn a wide variety of skills using discrete-trial teaching. However, those skills will not be helpful to the student in the long term unless they can use those skills in a variety of different everyday situations. Teachers need to know how to ensure that learning lasts – that is, to teach mathematical skills in such a way that children will still be able to use their skills for months or even years after the termination of their formal teaching sessions, and in a variety of situations.

When the student can use a target skill taught during discrete-trial teaching, at other times or in places different from the initial teaching environment, without the skill having to be re-taught completely in those new times or places, the student has made a generalization. In this chapter, we will distinguish between an instructional setting – the setting in which the initial instruction occurs – and the generalization setting – any place or situation that differs in some important way from the instructional setting and in which a demonstration of the learnt skill is anticipated.

Generalization of skills is a crucial outcome. For many of us, once we have learnt a new skill for the first time, it is relatively easy to perform that skill in other places, at different times, and with different people. However, for many children and adults with a developmental disability, generalization often does not automatically happen, particularly for those with an autism diagnosis. Generalization may have to be very systematically planned for and a lot of hard work may have to be put into helping the student use their skills in a multitude of everyday situations, including: in different settings, with different teachers, and with different teaching materials. Teachers of students with a developmental disability should not expect that generalization will occur spontaneously. Rather, they should plan systematically to ensure that generalization happens.

Much of the teaching using the approach in this book will involve generalization. When a student has mastered any skill during discrete-trial teaching sessions, we should ensure that he or she can use the skill functionally in novel contexts. In this chapter, we will explain how you can plan for and promote generalized behavior change. We will focus on five main types of generalization:

- Response maintenance (generalization across time)
- Generalization across people
- Generalization across settings
- Stimulus generalization
- Response generalization

Response maintenance

Response maintenance refers to the extent to which a student is able to continue to demonstrate a particular skill after a portion, or all, of the intervention responsible for the student learning the skill initially has been removed. Sometimes, response maintenance is referred to as generalization across time. For example, initially Monty learns to recognize numeral cards 1–10 correctly (see lesson plan A2.4: Numeral Recognition) provided that he receives a token after each correct answer. Six months after he was initially taught the skill, he can still recognize all of the numeral cards correctly even when the token board is no longer being used. In this example, response maintenance can be said to have occurred because Monty is demonstrating a previously acquired skill over time in a situation where the frequency and the intensity of reinforcement have been reduced substantially from the level used to originally teach the skill. Table 7.1 summarizes some key guidelines for teaching so that response maintenance occurs. These guidelines are explained in the text that follows.

Table 7.1   Guidelines for teaching so that response maintenance occurs

1.	Teach skills so that the student's behavior is reinforced in the generalization setting:
	• Select reinforcers that are present in everyday settings
	• Teach skills that are necessary and relevant for the student's life
	• Teach skills to a high level of competence
2.	Vary how and when reinforcement is delivered:
	• Reinforce frequently at the beginning of teaching, and gradually fade (reduce)
	• Gradually build in delays to reinforcement
3.	Teach skills that can subsequently be used to teach more complex skills
4.	Practice earlier achieved targets at regular intervals
5.	Teach loosely

Teach skills so that the student's behavior is reinforced in the generalization setting

Select reinforcers that are present in everyday settings

Reinforcers that are likely to be present in the student's natural, everyday settings should be used. For example, food reinforcers or other tangible items like the iPad are not likely to be present with sufficient frequency to maintain learnt skills outside of the instructional setting and their use is not necessarily socially appropriate, especially in the long term. The student will also learn very quickly to discriminate between those environments in which they receive these reinforcers and those in which they do not. The student's newly learnt skills may rapidly decrease in new environments and eventually drop off altogether.

To avoid this problem, you could gradually transfer the use of food reinforcers or the iPad, for example, to reinforcers you would find in the natural environment. In Chapter 5, we described the importance of teachers always praising children for correct responding during discrete-trial teaching even if they are also delivering other tangible reinforcers at the same time. Praise is ubiquitous in generalization settings – anyone can offer praise to a child and it is easy to do. Teachers should also always be on the lookout for other naturally occurring reinforcers. If the student is in a class where the teacher already uses a star chart or similar token economy system, every effort should be made to work toward using these existing systems for delivering reinforcers.

Teach skills that are necessary and relevant for the student's life

When a student is taught skills and language that will be relevant to their lives, response maintenance is much more likely. For example, for a student with language delay, when choosing new vocabulary to teach them you would want to teach language that would be directly useful to them. If a student lives by the seaside and goes for regular walks along the beach with their parents, the word 'shell' may crop up regularly in conversation and subsequently be more likely to be maintained when the student receives attention and praise from the parents in this situation. If a student with language delay who lives in the city, however, is taught the word 'shell', there would likely be fewer opportunities for the student to practice using the word in the generalization setting and for this skill to be subsequently reinforced and maintained.

In Mathematics Recovery, the range of skills to be taught has been selected to represent those skills that should be relevant in children's everyday lives (see Table 2.2, Chapter 2 for the scope of teaching activities across the key topics). For example, finger counting is a target to teach because virtually all neurotypical children seem to go through a period where they count using their fingers in more, or less, sophisticated ways. As there are many opportunities for a student to count with their fingers during their everyday experiences outside of their teaching sessions, this is a skill that is likely to produce naturally occurring reinforcement for the student at least on some occasions, and counting would be more likely to be maintained across time.

Teach skills to a high level of competence

Sometimes, a student may learn a skill in the instructional setting but not well enough for other people to notice in the generalization setting. For example, a student may have been taught to name each numeral accurately, but they might typically need between five and 10 seconds to do this. If later they are seated on the carpet with their peers while the class teacher holds up flash cards depicting numerals for the children to identify, the student may not be able to respond quickly enough for the teacher to notice that they can do the task and subsequently to praise them for doing so. One solution would be for the teacher to focus on making sure that the skill is much more fluent (fast, as well as accurate) so that the student can respond at the same rate or even faster than the other children.

Vary how and when reinforcement is delivered

In Chapter 5, we described how important it is that the student receives consistent, unambiguous and immediate consequences when they learn new skills. Such recommendations, however, can also be problematic in the long term as they can work against the generalization and maintenance of skills. There are two main ways in which teachers can start to adjust how reinforcement is delivered in the instructional setting so that it is similar to what the student will encounter in the generalization setting:

1. Reinforce frequently at the beginning of teaching, and gradually fade (reduce)
2. Gradually build in delays to reinforcement

Reinforce frequently at the beginning of teaching, and gradually fade (reduce)

Continuous reinforcement, i.e., reinforcement after each correct response, is the most effective way to teach a new skill for the very first time (see Chapter 5). However, when the skill has been established it is important to start providing reinforcement on a more intermittent basis. For example, a reinforcer may be provided after every fifth response or after every eighth response. Reinforcers should follow some occurrences of the target skill but not all occurrences, and the student should not be able to predict which responses will be followed by reinforcers. This is called an intermittent schedule of reinforcement. Research has shown that new skills will be maintained for much longer periods of time when teachers use this method as a part of their teaching protocol (e.g., Cooper et al.,

2007; Lattal & Neef, 1996). If reinforcement is not delivered every time that the target skill is demonstrated, the student cannot be sure which of their correct responses will result in a reward. As a result, to ensure that they receive the reward at all, the student strives to provide correct responses with all of his or her relevant skills all the time.

As described in Chapter 5, it may also be important to reduce the intensity of the reinforcement as teaching progresses. Although a student may receive exuberant praise from their teacher the very first time they demonstrate a new skill, it would be impractical to continue to deliver reinforcement in this way indefinitely. Parents instinctively reduce the frequency and intensity of praise during the teaching of early skills. For example, when a child is very young and is first being toilet trained, parents would likely provide high energy praise every single time that the child uses the toilet appropriately. As the child becomes more adept at using the skill, however, parents would start to expect that the child uses the toilet appropriately without being praised every single time. Eventually, when the skill is well established, reinforcement would tail off altogether.

Gradually build in delays to reinforcement

We also described in Chapter 5 how important it is when first learning a new skill that a student is given a reinforcer *immediately* upon the occurrence of a correct response. This not only helps the student to remember the correct response and repeat it in the future, it also reduces the likelihood that an intervening response will occur between the target skill and reinforcement. For example, if a student recognizes a numeral card correctly, and there is a pause of a few seconds during which time the student starts to shout, if the student is provided with reinforcement at that point for touching the correct numeral card, it may be the shouting that is reinforced and strengthened and not selecting the correct named numeral from a set of numerals. However, when a skill is more established, it is also important that the student becomes accustomed to receiving reinforcement on a more delayed basis, as again this is more typical of how reinforcement is delivered in natural settings.

Teachers can gradually increase the response-to-reinforcement delay. For example, a student may receive a reward after one minute of working which coincides with them completing around 12 trials of numeral identification. When the student has shown aptitude with this short delay, the delay could be gradually increased to between two and five minutes, and then between five and 10 minutes (e.g., they get time on the iPad after they have completed their numeracy session). Even longer delays could eventually be built in, such that the student receives their reward at morning break time or during lunch time. It is important that each time a delayed reward is delivered, the teacher explains to the student why it is that they are receiving the reward and, if possible, specifically for which skills they are receiving the reward (e.g., 'I loved how you did your counting earlier. You can have five extra minutes' play time today'). This will help the student understand why they received the reward, and what they need to do more of in the future to continue to receive the rewards.

Using token economy boards (see Chapter 4) can be a highly effective way to help the student understand and tolerate increased delays to reinforcement. For example, a student could earn tokens and praise intermittently during a session for correct responding, but then not exchange the tokens for a main reinforcer until break time or the end of the day. In this way, the receipt of tokens helps to bridge the gap between correct responding and receiving the main reward. Again, this idea is commonly used with children generally. Parents may have a star chart on the wall and give their child pocket money at the end of the week if they have received stars daily for tidying their room, doing their homework, and such. Some schools use a system where the children save points earned throughout the week for working hard during their lessons to get time to play on a Friday afternoon.

Teach skills that can subsequently be used to teach more complex skills

We described in Chapter 2 how the original Mathematics Recovery program is very well structured and systematic: numeracy targets are organized both horizontally (different groups of activities within the same ability level key topics) and vertically. Thus, there are progressive stages of difficulty so that certain teaching activities would not be introduced until a student has demonstrated proficiency with earlier prerequisite skills. This is also an important component of the program that can help to facilitate response maintenance for children who are following the program set out in this book.

A teacher may decide to teach Backward Number Word Sequences (BNWS) during the Emergent Phase (see lesson plan A1.2: Copying and Saying Short Backward Number Word Sequences) because they know that fluency with BNWS by itself is an important skill. That is, they know that it is important that if a student is asked to say number words backwards from 7 to 4, they are able to do so correctly. Another reason to teach BNWS is that this skill is crucial for teaching other, more complex skills. For example, a student cannot learn how to do subtraction unless they know first how to complete BNWS tasks where they start saying number words backwards from different numbers. If a student has been taught to 'count backwards from 8 to 3', for example, they could then use this skill to work out, through saying number words backwards, that 8 subtract 3 is 5.

When initial skills continue to be used regularly in the teaching of new skills, and are used repeatedly, response maintenance is also more likely to occur because the student is still practicing using the earlier skills in the demonstration of the more complex skill, and is receiving reinforcement for doing so.

Practice earlier achieved targets at regular intervals

Sometimes, for children with developmental disabilities, the approaches described previously are not quite enough to ensure that response maintenance occurs. For example, you may find that you are teaching the skill of 'numeral identification for numerals 6–9' for quite a while as the student is finding it difficult to learn to discriminate between numerals 6 and 9, or 6 and 8. If your goal is to teach these numerals to mastery, you may be teaching for many trials before you reach that goal. In this situation, you would not want the student to forget the earlier targets while you are focusing on teaching the new discrimination. You would not want them to forget how to identify numerals 1–5 during the days or weeks that you are practicing numerals 6–9.

Therefore, earlier targets should be 'practiced' at regular intervals so that the student does not forget them. It may be helpful to set aside time every week or every month for a 'maintenance session' where you specifically practice those skills taught that have not yet been incorporated into the teaching of more complex skills. You could document the student's maintenance of skills by using a logbook or data sheet where you record the date that you practiced the skill and whether or not the student was incorrect or correct. An example of a data sheet to keep track of whether or not a skill is being maintained over time (i.e., a maintenance checklist) can be downloaded from the website accompanying this book. If the student starts to get many incorrect responses on a skill that was previously thought to be learnt, you may have to reintroduce teaching it more formally again using the strategies outlined in Chapters 4–6.

In Chapter 6, we discussed the importance of using distractor trials during error correction procedures. One very useful way to ensure that older targets are maintained is to use previously mastered targets interspersed with new targets that you are teaching. Thus, you could try using some of the older numeracy targets during these distractor trials. Some teachers also like to take this one step further and use the '80% easy and 20% difficult rule'. When teaching a specific target at the table, a teacher may also have a 'mastered' or 'maintenance' pile of cards which specify instructions for numeracy skills that have been previously mastered. These mastered targets are considered the 'easy' tasks, whereas the acquisition targets are considered the 'difficult' tasks. In interspersing difficult tasks with easier tasks, a teacher tries to ensure that at least 80% of their teaching time is spent on the easier (mastered) tasks, and only 20% of their time is spent on the more difficult (acquisition) tasks.

There are two main benefits to this 80/20 approach. First, it helps to ensure that response maintenance occurs as it is less likely that any previously taught targets will be forgotten as they are practiced regularly. Second, some students may struggle to remain motivated when they are being taught new skills due to the likelihood of higher errors, corresponding lesser degrees of reinforcement and more effort being required. As with errorless teaching, described in Chapter 6, the 80/20 rule can help to ensure lots of success and keep the student well motivated during teaching sessions.

Teach loosely

The final guideline for teaching so that response maintenance occurs is to *teach loosely*. In Chapter 5, we described how important it is, during the initial stages of teaching, that teachers always use the same instructions as those written into the lesson plans. This is an example of early numeracy skills being established first in the instructional setting, using fairly restricted, simplified, and consistent conditions (e.g., sitting at the same table, using the same instructions, using the same teaching materials). It is unlikely, however, that children will be able to continue to use their skills after formal teaching has been terminated if teachers always restrict their teaching procedures in this way.

A basic strategy for promoting response maintenance is to make the instructional setting as similar as possible to the generalization setting (home, community, etc.). One way of doing this is to 'teach loosely' (e.g., see Cooper et al., 2007, p. 633). This is when teachers vary as many of the non-critical features of an antecedent stimulus (verbal instruction, visual cue, etc.) as they can, within and across teaching sessions. For example, a student who has a history of receiving reinforcement for complying with a teacher's directions when they are given in a loud authoritative voice and the teacher is sitting opposite them at a table, may not follow the directions if a teacher speaks more quietly or is sitting next to them. Loose teaching in this context might involve the teacher making a conscious effort to vary their tone of voice, give some instructions while standing, while sitting, and while looking away from the child, at different times of the day, when the student is alone or in a small group, and so on. Irrespective of the presence or absence of any of these non-critical variables, reinforcement should be dependent on the student following the content of the teacher's statements, and nothing else. Baer (1999, p. 24) provided several suggestions to teachers for teaching loosely:

- Use at least two teachers (see generalization across people, below).
- Teach in at least two places (see generalization across settings, below).
- Teach from a variety of positions – sometimes standing, sometimes sitting.
- Vary your tone of voice.
- Present the teaching materials from different positions – sometimes from the left side, sometimes the right, using one hand, sometimes the other.
- Dress quite differently on different days – sometimes casual clothes, sometimes more formal dress.
- Use different reinforcers (see Chapter 4).
- Vary the room lighting – sometimes bright, sometimes dim.
- Vary the noise in the room – sometimes noisy, sometimes quiet.
- Vary pictures/furniture in the room, and vary their locations.
- Vary the times of the day that the student has their teaching sessions.

Changing these non-critical aspects of the instructional setting and teaching procedures should be done as frequently and as unpredictably as possible.

Some of these suggestions have been explained elsewhere in the book and some are described in more detail in the sections below. Cooper et al. (2007) emphasize that the important point is not that teachers need to diligently vary all of these factors for every skill being taught, but that building in a reasonable degree of 'looseness' should be an important consideration for programming for generalization, rather than just assuming that generalization will automatically happen.

Generalization across people

After a lot of hard work during a structured discrete-trial teaching session, Mrs Jones, the teacher, has managed to teach Robert to consistently respond '1-2-3-4-5' when she asks, 'Count from 1 up to 5' (see lesson plan A1.1: Copying and Saying Short Forward Number Word Sequences). However, when Mrs Jones is away from work, and another teacher takes the lesson and gives the same instruction, Robert does not seem to know how to do this. A more long-term goal then needs to be that Robert can give the same response when Mrs Beech, the temporary teacher, asks him, or when Mr Rees, the paraprofessional asks him, or indeed whenever any other adult asks him to demonstrate this skill. Generalization across people occurs when the student is able to demonstrate the skill with a person other than the person who conducted the initial teaching of the skill.

If the student is receiving teaching sessions at school, try not to have only one teacher working with them. Arrange the timetable so that a few different teachers and paraprofessionals deliver the sessions across the week. You can also facilitate generalization across people by notifying the student's parents about newly learnt skills. Ask the parents if they, and other family members, would like to practice these newly learnt skills with their son or daughter on a regular basis. There needs to be clear feedback mechanisms between school and home so that parents can be quickly alerted when the student masters new skills during structured teaching and these can be practiced at home.

If the student is receiving teaching sessions at home and predominantly just one parent/carer delivers the sessions, try to arrange it so that other family members deliver some teaching or ask relevant questions at least some of the time. Involving grandparents, aunts, uncles and siblings can be a fun way to ensure that generalization across people occurs.

Generalization across settings

Saeeda is a 14-year-old student with a diagnosis of autism who attends an autism classroom in a special school. She completes all of her taught sessions at her quiet, low-distraction workstation. Her workstation faces away from the main classroom and has a bookcase on one side and a board to the other which provide screening from the rest of the class. Her sessions are very successful, and she quickly learns new skills. The teacher decides to move Saeeda to a different table in the classroom that does not have screening. When the teacher asks Saeeda to respond on the basis of previously learnt skills, she does not answer. She is too busy looking to see what the other students in the class are doing.

The teacher quickly decides that it would be better for Saeeda if, in future, she only conducts her sessions at the workstation. However, this may lead to a generalization problem. Generalization across settings is when the student is able to demonstrate learnt skills in a variety of locations different from those in which the initial teaching occurred.

If the student is receiving taught sessions at school, try to arrange teaching opportunities where the student can practice previously learnt skills in lots of locations different from those in which the skill was originally taught. It may be helpful to start by varying locations just within the same room in which they usually receive their sessions. For example, if a student has been taught to identify numerals at their workstation in the classroom, have them identify numerals in a variety of different settings *within the classroom* first, such as sitting on a different chair in the classroom, or sitting on the carpet with their peers. Be patient and systematic with this. It may take several sessions for the student to get used to responding in different settings within the same classroom.

When the student can consistently generalize to different places within their usual classroom, you could check for generalization to different places around the school. Can they still identify numerals if you take the numeral cards into the school hall, into the playground, and so on? You should be aiming to practice skills during recess and lunch time in the playground, the cafeteria, and any other available settings in the school. As with generalization across people, contact the student's parents to ask them to generalize different skills to the home setting and in the community.

If the child is receiving taught sessions at home and predominantly you deliver teaching in just one location (e.g., sitting in a particular place at the dining room table), have the child start to practice skills in different locations in the home. Start with varying the locations only slightly and, if possible, in the same room in which initial teaching occurred (e.g., different seats around the dining room table), but gradually extend teaching to different rooms in the home. For example, have the child count tokens on the floor in their bedroom, at the dining table, and in the play room. When you are confident that the child can use the skill anywhere in the home, you can generalize to other appropriate community settings such as the park, or in a restaurant.

One of the key aspects to generalization across people and generalization across settings is that staff, parents and caregivers allow the student to use the skills that have been targeted during teaching when naturally occurring opportunities arise – for example, counting out four apples to put in a bag when shopping in a supermarket, or looking out for a numeral on a bus while waiting at a bus stop. There is also some overlap here with the next topic – stimulus generalization.

Stimulus generalization

In Chapter 5, we described that the first part of the discrete trial is called an antecedent which 'sets up' or 'cues' a response. An antecedent can be a discrete event such as a visual or auditory stimulus. It is important that, for a given skill, the student is taught to respond correctly to more than one example of an antecedent stimulus condition. This is called stimulus generalization. The sections below describe how to arrange teaching so that stimulus generalization occurs across visual cues, for example by using different teaching materials, and across verbal instructions.

Varying antecedent teaching materials

Many different mathematical teaching materials (flashcards, counters, etc.) can be considered to be an antecedent visual stimulus, the presence of which functions as an antecedent that signals to a student that they should respond in a particular way. For example, a teacher may hold up a picture domino card with three dots on, and this will lead the student to say, without counting, 'three' when they see the dots (see lesson plan A4.1: Ascribing Numerosity to Patterns and Random Arrays). It is important, however, that the student does not learn to respond with 'three' *only* when they see the three dots, but they can also say 'three' if they see a picture with three ducks or if they see a picture card with three stars. There are now more stimuli that lead to the same response (saying 'three'). This is an example of stimulus generalization, as indicated in Figure 7.1.

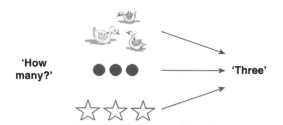

Figure 7.1 An example of stimulus generalization using different teaching materials

One of the main aims of stimulus generalization is that a student is able to demonstrate a particular skill when they are provided with untaught (novel) stimulus examples. That is, using the previous example, if a student is shown any picture of three items they would be able to say 'three' even if they have not seen the exact configuration of the three items before. With many children with a developmental disability, it is important to remember that the transfer of this skill may not automatically happen but may need to be systematically planned. It is impossible for an educator to teach a student to respond to absolutely every possible example of different manifestations of teaching materials. Cooper et al. (2007, p. 627) describe a general strategy called 'teaching sufficient stimulus examples', which involves teaching a student to respond to a subset of all of the possible stimulus examples and then assessing (probing) their performance on some untaught examples.

An example of what this process might look like for teaching a student to say 'three' when shown an untaught picture of three items is illustrated in Figure 7.2.

Prerequisite skill	**When asked, 'how many?' and a card with three dots is presented, Jane consistently says 'three' (i.e., the skill is mastered)**
Generalization probe	Mrs Brown: Points to a picture card with three ducks, and asks 'How many?' Jane: 'Quack quack' **(incorrect response)**
Instructional setting	• Using discrete-trial teaching (DTT), Mrs Brown teaches Jane to say 'three' when she sees the picture card with three ducks • Mrs Brown checks to see that Jane can still remember to say 'three' in the presence of three dots (response maintenance)
Generalization probe	Mrs Brown: Points to a picture card with three stars, and asks 'How many?' Jane: 'Star' **(incorrect response)**
Instructional setting	• Using DTT, Mrs Brown teaches Jane to say 'three' when she sees the picture card with three stars • Mrs Brown checks to see that Jane can still remember to say 'three' in the presence of three dots and three ducks (response maintenance)
Generalization probe	Mrs Brown: Points to a picture card with three pigs, and asks, 'How many?' Jane: 'Three' **(correct response)**
Generalization probe	Mrs Brown: Points to a picture card with three cats, and asks 'How many?' Jane: 'Three' **(correct response)**
Generalization probe	Mrs Brown: Points to a picture card with three cars, and asks 'How many?' Jane: 'Three' **(correct response)**
The skill is generalized after three consecutive correct responses, using untaught (novel) teaching materials	

Figure 7.2   Example of a generalization probe procedure for stimulus generalization using different teaching materials

In Figure 7.2, the generalization of Jane's ability to recognize and label the quantity of three was assessed by asking Jane to respond to several configurations of the same quantity to which no instruction had been provided (the generalization probe). When the generalization probe resulted in Jane responding correctly on three separate occasions to untaught examples, then her teacher stopped teaching. However, if Jane had continued to perform poorly on the generalization probe, her teacher would have continued to teach additional examples before again assessing how she performed with the untaught examples. When a student can consistently respond correctly to untaught examples (at least on three separate occasions), this can be considered to be representative of the full range of possible stimulus examples, even if they have not all been formally taught.

There are at least two contexts in which different instructional examples can be taught to generalization. The first is when the specific *item* taught is varied, as with the previous example. The second is when the *stimulus context* in which the item is taught is varied. For example, when asking 'how many?', the teacher may present dots that are arranged in a top-down (vertical) format, in a left to right (horizontal) format, or in a random array format. Not only can the quantity be arranged using various 2D (picture) representations, they can also be arranged using different arrangements in a 3D format – for example, three cups on the table, three sweets in a parent's hand.

In most cases, the more examples the teacher uses during teaching sessions, the more likely it is that the student will be able to generalize and answer correctly to untaught examples. The actual number of examples that must be taught before generalization happens will vary very much, depending on the individual student and on the complexity of the skill that is being taught. Sometimes teaching just two or three stimulus examples may be enough to produce generalization, however teachers should be prepared to teach many more.

Varying antecedent verbal instructions

In Chapter 5, we provided some guidelines for delivering the antecedent effectively during discrete-trial teaching. We recommended, for example, that in the instructional setting during the early stages of teaching, verbal instructions be kept simple and concise, and the same word or phrase should be used consistently during early teaching. However, we emphasized that, as the student progresses and learns new skills in the instructional setting, teachers should aim to use more complex natural language and should start to vary the instructions that they use. Figure 7.3 provides an example of stimulus generalization where the stimulus altered is the verbal instruction rather than the teaching materials (as in the examples provided previously).

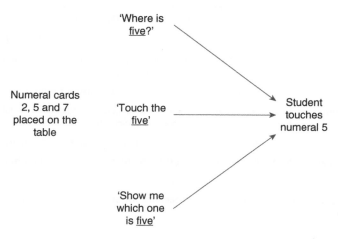

Figure 7.3 An example of stimulus generalization with different verbal instructions

The process of teaching the student to generalize across different verbal instructions is the same as described previously for generalization across teaching materials. A student would be taught to respond to a subset of different verbal instructions that should elicit the same response, and then assessed to see if they could follow some untaught antecedent instructions. An example of what this process might look like for teaching a student to touch a numeral 5 when varied verbal instructions are used is illustrated in Figure 7.4.

Prerequisite skill	**When asked 'Touch five' and a card with the numeral 5 is presented in an array with two other numeral cards, Jane is able to consistently touch the numeral 5.**	
Generalization probe	Mrs Brown:	Three numeral cards are placed on the table including the numeral 5, 'Where is 5?'
	Jane:	**'Five' (incorrect response, Jane just repeats back the word 'five' but does not select a numeral card)**
Instructional setting	• Using discrete-trial teaching (DTT), Mrs Brown teaches Jane to select numeral card 5 after the instruction, 'Where is 5?' • Mrs Brown checks to see that Jane can still select the numeral 5 in a random array of cards when asked, 'Touch 5'.	
Generalization probe	Mrs Brown:	Three numeral cards are placed on the table, including the numeral 5, 'Show me which one is 5'
	Jane:	Non-response for 10 seconds **(incorrect response)**
Instructional setting	• Using DTT, Mrs Brown teaches Jane to select numeral card 5 after the instruction, 'Show me which one is 5' • Mrs Brown checks to see that Jane can still remember to select 5 in a random array of cards when asked, 'Touch 5' and 'Where is 5?'	
Generalization probe	Mrs Brown:	Three numeral cards are placed on the table, including the numeral 5, 'Put your hand on 5'
	Jane:	Touches numeral 5 **(correct response)**
Generalization probe	Mrs Brown:	Three numeral cards are placed on the table, including the numeral 5, 'Select number 5'
	Jane:	Touches numeral 5 **(correct response)**
Generalization probe	Mrs Brown:	Three numeral cards are placed on the table, including the numeral 5, 'Which one of these cards has the number 5 on?'
	Jane:	Touches numeral 5 **(correct response)**

The skill is generalized after three consecutive correct responses, using untaught (novel) verbal instructions.

Figure 7.4   Example of a generalization probe procedure for stimulus generalization using different verbal instructions

In this example, Jane's teacher has gradually used more complex and varied language to elicit the same response. Jane no longer needs to rely on simple and concise wording being used every time, and now is in a much better position to be able to respond to more natural language that she will come across in her environment (at home, in the community, etc.).

Response generalization

Response generalization, instead of describing when different stimuli lead to the same response, is when the *same* stimulus leads to *different* responses that mean the same thing as (i.e., is functionally equivalent to) the original response. Response generalization is also sometimes called generalization across behaviors. A common everyday example is when toddlers say 'mama' when they see their mother. As time goes by, and as they get older, they may start to say 'mummy' and use 'mama' and 'mummy' interchangeably. Eventually the child learns to say the slightly more grown up 'mom' or 'mum', especially when they are in the company of their friends, but use 'mummy' when they are at home where they do not need to be concerned about their friends teasing them. This is response generalization because, although the stimulus (mother) remained the same, there is now a greater number of responses to that stimulus.

Response generalization could be said to have occurred when the same stimulus (e.g., instruction, visual cue) leads to a variety of responses. For example, if you were to clap five times and ask the student, 'How many claps?', an example of response generalization would occur if sometimes the student says 'five', and on another occasion the student says 'five claps', and on yet another occasion they say, 'I can hear five claps'. If they can respond differently to the same instruction, it is likely that they have generalized across responses and that the skill (saying 'five') has not simply been rote learnt (e.g., like with memorizing saying the alphabet).

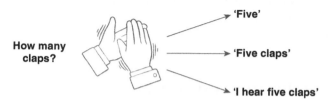

Figure 7.5 An example of response generalization

We described in the previous section how instruction that provides practice with sufficient stimulus examples helps to promote stimulus generalization. This is also a relevant concept for response generalization, where it may be useful to teach sufficient *response* examples. One of the easiest ways to encourage response generalization for verbal responses is to provide verbal feedback to the student after they give a correct response that models a different way of responding.

For example:

Teacher:	(Teacher claps five times) 'How many claps?'
Child:	'Five'
Teacher:	'That's right. **Five claps. You hear five claps**'

If the student then starts to use a phrase different from the one they had initially been taught or different from the one which they usually use, the teacher could give a descriptive phrase related to the change of phrase. For example, if the student usually responds with 'five' when asked, 'how many claps?' and instead says, 'I hear five claps' after hearing that phrase modeled for them, the teacher could respond with, 'You're right, you hear five claps. What a lovely long sentence you have used.' Reinforcing the use of different phrases in this way helps to increase the frequency of using other, more varied responses to instructions.

For some non-verbal responses, the teacher can encourage a variety of different responses that are functionally equivalent. For example, in the Making Auditory Patterns to Match Spatial Patterns teaching activity (lesson plan A4.3) the teacher could hold up a domino card with six dots, and ask, 'Bang the drum to show me how many dots', and the student bangs a drum six times. The student could, on some occasions, be given a tambourine to strike or a musical triangle to use. Each of the responses would produce functionally similar outcomes (making an auditory pattern to match a spatial pattern) and yet all of the responses look very different from one another. Similarly, for Counting Items in One Collection (lesson plan A3.1) a student could be taught to point, using an index finger, to each item as they count, to tap lightly on each item as they count, or to push each item forward slightly as they count. Again, the responses are functionally similar (they all demonstrate proficiency with counting with one-to-one correspondence) and yet they all look quite different from one another.

Generalization: an intermixed concept

For simplicity's sake, we have described some of the main forms of generalized behavior change independently, under their own subheadings, to emphasize their main defining characteristics (generalization across people, generalization across settings, etc.). In practice, it is more usual that different forms of generalization occur in combination and are represented in the same instance.

Cooper et al. (2007) refer to generalization as being an 'intermixed concept' (p. 621). For example, although it is possible that response maintenance can occur without generalization across people or across settings (i.e., the student is able to count in the classroom with the initial teacher that taught the skill one year after token reinforcement has been faded), this would not be a desirable outcome by itself. It is common for different forms of generalized behavior change to co-occur in the same situation. For example, in Monday's lesson (the instructional setting), Mrs Smith uses discrete-trial teaching and token board reinforcement to teach Barnabas to point and count to five red counters on the table. One month later (response maintenance) in the dining hall (generalization across settings), the school cook (generalization across people) asks Barnabas how many chicken nuggets he has on his plate (generalization across stimuli). Barnabas prods each chicken nugget with his fork as he counts (response generalization).

Using a generalization checklist

When a student has learnt skills in the instructional setting, teaching in the generalization setting can begin. As described, there are many different types of generalization and it can be difficult to remember exactly what needs to be done. The lesson plans provide a few examples of generalization that you can focus on for a given skill. However, it may be useful for some teachers to focus on a more detailed approach to planning for generalization. A blank template of a checklist that you can use to monitor generalization across different subcategories (for both home and school settings) can be downloaded from the website accompanying this book. Figure 7.6 illustrates how the checklist can be completed and individualized for a student in a school setting who is learning to count visible items up to 20 (from lesson plan A3.1).

You can be flexible in deciding where you start teaching using the checklist and which substeps to work on formally. As long as the student accomplishes the main goals (1 and 2), the skill can be considered generalized even if you do not systematically work through all the substeps. For some children, generalization will occur very quickly, while for others you may need to specifically train every substep until a skill can be considered generalized. You will notice that there is not a goal for response generalization on the checklist. If the student accomplishes goals 1 and 2, response generalization should occur naturally. Using the example in Figure 7.6, responses such as counting out drinks at snack time or chairs in the dining hall are different from counting out counters on the table during structured teaching settings. If the student does struggle with doing this, you could practice response generalization more specifically using the suggestions described previously.

GENERALIZATION PLAN CHECKLIST	
Lesson plan A3.1: Counting Items in One Collection using up to 20 counters	
1. Skill used with different staff members, peers, family members, and any other persons in natural settings and with natural cues	
Tick when generalized	**Practice skill:**
√	**With different people in a structured teaching session** Place counters on the table – counting with 2 paraprofessionals, class teacher, and peer at their workstation
√	**In different places in the room where the original teaching occurred** Sitting on the carpet and counting counters; sitting at different tables in the classroom
	In different rooms Counting in the dining hall, in the music room and in the playground
	In the community Counting on the minibus; counting in the café
	Using more natural language for instructions Place counters down, use varied language to cue counting; e.g., How many do you see? Count how many counters you see on the table
2. Skill practiced with various sets of objects and pictures	
Tick when generalized	**Practice skill:**
√	**With different objects at the table where teaching usually occurs** Use different colored counters; teddy bears; balls; pencils, etc.
√	**With different objects in natural settings** Counting cups needed at snack time; counting tables in the dinner hall; counting swings in the playground; counting books on a bookshelf
	With photos (if applicable) Counting number of people in a family photo; number of trees in a photo
	With pictures in a book (if applicable) Use different number counting books up to 20

Figure 7.6   An example of a partially completed checklist for generalization in school settings

The benefits of generalization

Some educators are initially nervous about using Systematic Instruction and discrete-trial teaching because of the structured nature of the teaching approach. Some of the most common criticisms of using discrete-trial teaching are:

1. Highly structured teaching environments impede the use of skills in everyday settings. For example, there may be concerns that even though a student can imitate their teacher in discrete-trial teaching sessions, they will not be able to imitate in non-teaching sessions with individuals other than their usual teacher or they will not be able to use spontaneous imitation in play.
2. Skills may occur only when the student hears the initial instruction given, so the spontaneous use of the skill is not generalized. For example, children cannot provide the correct number word unless they hear the specific instruction, 'How many?'
3. Children will only maintain skills if, for most responses, they continue to receive tangible or edible (i.e., artificial) reinforcers.
4. Responses are learnt as isolated skills and are not representative of natural adult–student or child–student interactions.

These criticisms are not problems with discrete-trial teaching in general. They are actually failures to promote generalization. In this chapter, we have focused on how to promote generalization.

8

Preparing to teach

Teaching numeracy to children with developmental disabilities requires some preparation in advance. This chapter describes how to lay the groundwork for instruction. There are four sections to this chapter. First, in the 'initial assessment' section, we will outline and describe an assessment procedure called the probe test that can be used to help teachers decide what should be the first areas to teach.

Second, once teachers know what they should be teaching they need to know how to teach the selected targets. Descriptions of the teaching procedures for each target skill are outlined in the lesson plans which can be downloaded from the website accompanying this book. All of the lesson plans follow the same structure. In the 'descriptions of the teaching activities' section, we will describe the structure of the lesson plans and how they can best be used.

Third, once teachers know how to teach target skills they need to know how to be sure that a skill is 'mastered' (learnt) and when to move on to the next skill to be taught. In this third section (ongoing assessment and data collection), we describe how to assess progress by taking data on the student's responses and how to use these data to check that the student is learning the skills being taught. If they are not, then it is advisable to revise instruction using some of the strategies described in this book (Chapters 4, 5 and 6).

The final section, 'Putting it all together: developing a plan for teaching', includes information from previous chapters to help teachers to consider important questions that they may need to answer before they start teaching using the lesson plans.

Initial assessment

As you set up the numeracy program, you will need to know how to select learning objectives for the student. Because no two students have the same strengths and weaknesses in their numeracy development, the initial selection of skills to teach needs to be based on each student's current skills and abilities. As described in Chapter 1, this is crucially important as teachers can sometimes struggle to know how best to assess students with developmental disabilities. If students are subsequently presented with a program that is either too easy for them or too difficult, this can result in difficulties as the student's behavior may become challenging in an attempt to avoid their teaching sessions. In this section, we present a framework for knowing how and when to select teaching activities so that you can start your teaching in the right place.

As described in Chapter 3, neurotypical students on the Mathematics Recovery program would usually be assessed using an interview where they answer questions about the strategies they would use to solve numeracy tasks. Many students with developmental disabilities, who may have concomitant language and communication difficulties, may find it difficult in an interview to understand the questions they are being asked or to be able to explain clearly the strategy they used to solve a task. We recommend instead using an assessment procedure called the probe test. Here, the teacher asks the student a series of probes (test questions) that correspond to the individual numeracy skills covered by the program, using simpler, more succinct instructions than those used in the original Mathematics Recovery assessment interview. A teacher who knows the student well is usually able to decide at which developmental Mathematics Recovery stage the student should be tested (Emergent, Perceptual or Figurative). However, on occasion a student may need to be tested across stages if they have an uneven numeracy profile. For example, a student in the Figurative Stage may have fairly advanced skills in numeral identification (i.e., be able to confidently name numerals up to 100) but not be able to say the short backward number word sequences 10–1 confidently (a target from the Emergent Stage).

We have developed probe checklists that present a list of the skills to assess that map exactly onto the skills described in the lesson plans. The probe checklists can subsequently be used as a framework for your initial assessment. Figure 8.1 shows an example probe checklist for a few of the skills from the Number Word Sequences key topic in the Emergent Stage. A full compilation of the probe checklists across the developmental phases can be downloaded from the website accompanying this book. The scoring system will be explained in the text below the figure.

Key Topic A1: Number Word Sequences from 1 to 20 Purpose: To check knowledge of forward number word sequences in the range 1 to 20 and backward number word sequences in the range 1 to 10	Probe date	✓ – independent correct response Ӽ – incorrect or prompted response
A1.1: Copying and Saying Short Forward Number Word Sequences (FNWSs)		
Copying		
a. **Let's count.** Teacher says the Forward Number Word sequence (FNWS) **1-2-3.** *Now your turn.* Student repeats	9.11.19	✓✓
b. Teacher says the FNWS from **4 to 6**, student repeats	9.11.19	✓Ӽ✓✓

c. Teacher says the FNWS from **7 to 10**, student repeats	9.11.19	χ✓✓✓
d. Teacher says the FNWS from **1 to 5**, student repeats	9.11.19	✓✓
e. Teacher says the FNWS from **6 to 10**, student repeats	9.11.19	✓✓
f. Teacher says the FNWS from **11 to 15**, student repeats	9.11.19	✓✓
g. Teacher says the FNWS from **15 to 20**, student repeats	9.11.19	✓✓
h. Teacher says the FNWS from **11 to 20**, student repeats	9.11.19	✓χ✓χ
Saying		
i. **Count from one up to ten.** Student says FNWS **1 to 10**	9.11.19	χχ
j. Student says the FNWS from **6 to 10** by themselves	9.11.19	χχ
k. Student says the FNWS from **8 to 15** by themselves		
l. Student says the FNWS from **15 to 20** by themselves		
m. Student says the FNWS from **1 to 20** by themselves		
A1.2: Copying and Saying Short Backward Number Word Sequences (BNWSs)		
Copying		
a. **Let's count backwards.** Teacher says the Backward Number Word sequence (BNWS) **3-2-1**. **Now your turn.** Student repeats	9.11.19	χχ
b. Teacher says the BNWS from **6 to 4**, student repeats	9.11.19	χχ
c. Teacher says the BNWS from **10 to 8**, student repeats.	9.11.19	χχ
d. Teacher says the BNWS from **4 to 1**, student repeats		
e. Teacher says the BNWS from **8 to 5**, student repeats		
f. Teacher says the BNWS from **10 to 7**, student repeats		
Saying		
g. **Count backwards from five to one.** Student says the BNWS from 5 to 1 by themselves		
h. Student says the BNWS from **8 to 3** by themselves		
i. Student says the BNWS from **10 to 5** by themselves		
j. Student says the BNWS from **10 to 1** by themselves		
A1.3: Saying Alternate Number Word Forwards and Backwards		
Alternate FNWS 1 to 10		
a. **Let's take turns to count. My turn first. One! Now your turn.** Alternate FNWS **1 to 5**, teacher starting with 1	9.11.19	χχ
b. **Now your turn to start with one.** Alternate FNWS **1 to 5**, student starting with 1	9.11.19	χχ
c. Alternate FNWS **1 to 10**, teacher starting with 1	9.11.19	χ

Figure 8.1 Probe checklist for a selection of skills from the Number Word Sequences key topic from the Emergent Stage

Probe test procedure

Some children are inconsistent with their responses. It is important to be sure that a student can demonstrate a particular skill on more than one occasion. Just because they can perform it once does not mean that that skill is in their repertoire. When assessing a skill, you need to provide a few opportunities to be sure that the student can reliably perform a response.

> Two consecutive correct responses = no further testing needed; skill can be considered known and that it does **not** need to be taught

Key Topic A1: Number Word Sequences from 1 to 20 Purpose: To check knowledge of forward number word sequences in the range 1 to 20 and backward number word sequences in the range 1 to 10	Probe date	✓ - independent correct response ✗– incorrect or prompted response
A1.1: Copying and Saying Short Forward Number Word Sequences (FNWSs)		
Copying		
a. *Let's count*. Teacher says the Forward Number Word sequence (FNWS) **1-2-3.** *Now your turn.* Student repeats	9.11.19	✓✓
b. Teacher says the FNWS from **4 to 6**, student repeats	9.11.19	✓✗✓✓
c. Teacher says the FNWS from **7 to 10**, student repeats	9.11.19	✗✓✓✓
d. Teacher says the FNWS from **1 to 5**, student repeats	9.11.19	✓✓
e. Teacher says the FNWS from **6 to 10**, student repeats	9.11.19	✓✓
f. Teacher says the FNWS from **11 to 15**, student repeats	9.11.19	✓✓
g. Teacher says the FNWS from **15 to 20**, student repeats	9.11.19	✓✓
h. Teacher says the FNWS from **11 to 20**, student repeats	9.11.19	✓✗✓✗
Saying		
i. *Count from one up to ten.* Student says FNWS **1 to 10**	9.11.19	✗✗
j. Student says the FNWS from **6 to 10** by themselves.	9.11.19	✗✗
k. Student says the FNWS from **8 to 15** by themselves		
l. Student says the FNWS from **15 to 20** by themselves		
m. Student says the FNWS from **1 to 20** by themselves		

> Two consecutive incorrect responses = no further testing needed; skill can be considered **not** known and it **will** need to be taught

Figure 8.2   Scoring procedure for two consecutive correct responses and two consecutive incorrect responses

In a probe testing session, the student is initially asked two questions corresponding to each skill. If the student answers both questions correctly, the skill is considered known to the student and does not need to be formally taught. After two consecutive correct responses, the teacher can also stop testing that skill. If two consecutive incorrect responses are given, the skill is considered not known and the student would need to be taught that skill. The teacher can also stop testing that skill after two consecutive incorrect responses. This scoring procedure is illustrated in Figure 8.2.

One correct and one incorrect on first two trials = two further probes needed

Key Topic A1: Number Word Sequences from 1 to 20	Probe date	✓- independent correct response χ – incorrect or prompted response
Purpose: To check knowledge of forward number word sequences in the range 1 to 20 and backward number word sequences in the range 1 to 10		
A1.1: Copying and Saying Short Forward Number Word Sequences (FNWSs)		
Copying		
a. *Let's count*. Teacher says the Forward Number Word sequence (FNWS) **1-2-3**. *Now your turn*. Student repeats	9.11.19	✓✓
b. Teacher says the FNWS from **4 to 6**, student repeats	9.11.19	✓χ✓✓
c. Teacher says the FNWS from **7 to 10**, student repeats	9.11.19	χ✓✓✓
d. Teacher says the FNWS from **1 to 5**, student repeats	9.11.19	✓✓
e. Teacher says the FNWS from **6 to 10**, student repeats	9.11.19	✓✓
f. Teacher says the FNWS from **11 to 15**, student repeats	9.11.19	✓✓
g. Teacher says the FNWS from **15 to 20**, student repeats	9.11.19	✓✓
h. Teacher says the FNWS from **11 to 20**, student repeats	9.11.19	✓χ✓χ
Saying		
i. *Count from one up to ten*. Student says FNWS **1 to 10**	9.11.19	χχ
j. Student says the FNWS from **6 to 10** by themselves	9.11.19	χχ
k. Student says the FNWS from **8 to 15** by themselves		
l. Student says the FNWS from **15 to 20** by themselves		
m. Student says the FNWS from **1 to 20** by themselves		

Three correct responses out of four = skill can be considered known and that it does **not** need to be taught

Two corrects out of four = skill can be considered **not** known and it **will** need to be taught

Figure 8.3 Scoring procedure if the student provides one correct and one incorrect response on the first two trials

In the case of one correct and one wrong answer, a third and fourth question are asked. If the student is correct on these additional questions (thereby achieving three correct questions out of four), the skill can be considered known, and that it does *not* need to be taught. However, if the student is correct on only one out of the two additional questions (thereby achieving two out of four correct responses in total), the skill should be considered *not* known sufficiently and time would need to be spent on teaching this skill. This scoring procedure is illustrated in Figure 8.3.

The probe test procedure and progressive stages of difficulty

As described in Chapter 3, numeracy targets are organized both horizontally (different groups of activities within the same ability level key topics) and vertically, where there are progressive stages of difficulty for teaching activities within each key topic. For example, in the Emergent Stage for the Number Word Sequences from 1 to 20 (NWSs) key topic, the teaching activities are listed in the following developmental sequence from least-to-most difficult:

1. Copying and saying short FNWSs
2. Copying and saying short BNWSs
3. Saying alternate number words forwards and backwards
4. Saying the next number word forwards
5. Saying the next number word backwards
6. Saying the number word after
7. Saying the number word before

In the Emergent Stage for the Counting Visible Items key topic, the teaching activities are listed in this developmental sequence:

1. Counting items in one collection (e.g., counting eight counters in a row)
2. Establishing a collection of given numerosity
3. Counting items in a row, forwards and backwards
4. Counting items of two collections
5. Counting items of two rows

This arrangement, of listing targets from least-to-most difficult, has some relevance for the probe test procedure for targets within each key topic.

Probe testing within a key topic

If the student is not correct on the first few listed skills at the top of the hierarchy, it is highly unlikely that they would be correct on the later skills. For example, if a student is not able to say short backward number word sequences, they would not probably be able to say next number word backward or what number word comes before. If the student is not able to count items in one collection, it should not be expected that they be able to count items in two rows. When testing the child, therefore, if they are not correct with skills for the first couple of teaching activities within each key topic, it is probably not worth spending time assessing further to see if they are correct on the later skills.

This idea also works in reverse. If you are working with a student who you think is fairly advanced with their knowledge of the key topic, you could start testing at the bottom of the list of skills and work backwards. For example, if you decide to start testing a student in the Number Words Sequences key topic in the Emergent Stage by asking them questions like 'What number comes after 16?' or 'What number comes before 13?' (see lesson plans A1.6 and A1.7), and they are able to answer quickly and confidently, you probably do not need to test the earlier targets in the hierarchy (saying short forward and backward number word sequences). It is highly unlikely that they would not be able to do this if they have the later skill.

The idea behind both of these suggestions was described in Chapter 7, where we described how initial skills in the hierarchy are always required for the demonstration of the later skills. Thus, there should be no need to test for later skills if the early skills are not present, and similarly no need to test for the early skills if the later skills are there.

Probe testing within each teaching activity

There are also progressive stages of difficulty within each teaching activity. For example, in the Copying and Saying Short Forward Number Word Sequences teaching activity (see Figure 8.4 below), the skills are listed in an order from repeating numbers 1 to 3 when the numbers are modeled to them (skill a, in Figure 8.4), to saying the NWS from 1 to 10 independently without a modeling prompt (skill i) and saying the NWS in the range of 1 to 20 (skill m). If the student is not able to do the earlier skills within each teaching activity, there is little point continuing to test the later skills. This idea is illustrated in Figure 8.4. After the student is incorrect on two consecutive tasks (i and j, in the example), we recommend that the teacher discontinues testing for that teaching activity.

If you are confident that the student is able to complete the later tasks within a teaching activity (e.g., saying FNWS 1 to 20 without a modeling prompt), you could start your testing there. If the student is correct, there is often no need to continue working backwards to test the earlier skills as they are usually considered to be prerequisites for the demonstration of the later skills. There are, however, sometimes caveats to this rule. For example, a student may be able to say the FNWS 1 to 20 (skill m), but may struggle with following the earlier instruction 'count from 8 to 15' (skill k), possibly because they hear this instruction less often and may not know to stop counting at 15. If you think that this may be the case for your student, it is probably best to do a few checks of the earlier skills just to make sure.

| Key Topic A1: Number Word Sequences from 1 to 20

Purpose: To check knowledge of forward number word sequences in the range 1 to 20 and backward number word sequences in the range 1 to 10 | Probe date | ✓ – independent correct response
✗– incorrect or prompted response |
|---|---|---|
| **A1.1: Copying and Saying Short Forward Number Word Sequences (FNWSs)** | | |
| Copying | | |
| a. **Let's count.** Teacher says the Forward Number Word sequence (FNWS) **1-2-3. Now your turn.** Student repeats | 9.11.19 | ✓✓ |
| b. Teacher says the FNWS from **4 to 6**, student repeats | 9.11.19 | ✓✗✓✓ |
| c. Teacher says the FNWS from **7 to 10**, student repeats | 9.11.19 | ✗✓✓✓ |
| d. Teacher says the FNWS from **1 to 5**, student repeats | 9.11.19 | ✓✓ |
| e. Teacher says the FNWS from **6 to 10**, student repeats | 9.11.19 | ✓✓ |
| f. Teacher says the FNWS from **11 to 15**, student repeats | 9.11.19 | ✓✓ |
| g. Teacher says the FNWS from **15 to 20**, student repeats | 9.11.19 | ✓✓ |
| h. Teacher says the FNWS from **11 to 20**, student repeats | 9.11.19 | ✓✗✓✗ |
| Saying | | |
| i. **Count from one up to ten.** Student says FNWS **1 to 10** | 9.11.19 | ✗✗ |
| j. Student says the FNWS from **6 to 10** by themselves | 9.11.19 | ✗✗ |
| k. Student says the FNWS from **8 to 15** by themselves | | |
| l. Student says the FNWS from **15 to 20** by themselves | | |
| m. Student says the FNWS from **1 to 20** by themselves | | |

Teacher stops probing after the student obtains two incorrect responses for two successive tasks

Figure 8.4 Scoring procedure for probe testing within each teaching activity

Guidelines for the initial assessment

There are two important questions that you need to bear in mind when assessing the student:

1. Is the student demonstrating the skill when asked by their teacher, or at some other time?
2. Is the student able to demonstrate the skill without help?

Is the student demonstrating the skill when asked by their teacher, or at some other time?

Sometimes students may be observed to demonstrate a skill when they are playing or otherwise engaged in a solitary activity. For example, they may name numerals when they are looking at a book by themselves or they may line up and count trains when they are playing on the floor. If this is the case, then you should not score the skill as correct on the checklist on the basis of this observation alone. The student still needs to be able to demonstrate the skill in a teaching situation. Using the previous example, the student would also need to be able to count counters when they are placed on the table, or to name numeral cards that a teacher holds up for them.

Is the student able to demonstrate the skill without help?

It is important during your assessment that you determine a student's proficiency without any help. For example, if you want to know whether the student is able to recognize and select the numeral 3 from a selection of cards on the table, be sure that you do not inadvertently prompt by glancing toward the correct card on the table (see Chapter 6, for a description of inadvertent prompts). If you want to see if a student can identify (i.e., name) a numeral correctly, be careful not to mouth the answer. You should only score correct on the checklist if the student performs the response independently. If the student requires any help at all, you should score as incorrect.

Selecting teaching programs

Once you have conducted the probe test, it is time to decide where to start teaching. From your list of ticks and crosses you can generate a list of prospective teaching programs from the lesson plans. This can include one target from each key topic within the developmental phase you are working on, but there should not be more than one target within the same key topic. For example, depending on how a student performs on the initial assessment, their first targets from the Emergent Stage could include:

1. Saying short FNWS from 1 to 10 (from the Number Word Sequences key topic)
2. Saying a number word sequence 1 to 5 forwards (from the Numerals 1 to 10 key topic)
3. Counting 5 counters in one collection (from the Counting Visible Items key topic)
4. Counting 1 to 3 fingers sequentially with fingers seen, using the preferred hand (from the Finger Patterns key topic)

You could start by choosing a target from just one or two key topics until you familiarize yourself with the teaching protocol. However, to maximize the student's progress, it is advisable to work toward teaching one target from each of the five or six key topics within each session. There are also some questions you may want to consider before you decide where to start teaching:

1. Does the student have the necessary prerequisite skills to be able to learn the skill?
2. Is the student likely to acquire the skill in a reasonable amount of time?
3. What impact will teaching the skill have on challenging behavior?

Does the student have the necessary prerequisite skills to be able to learn the skill?

As described earlier, you will want to introduce the skills in the order in which they appear in the lesson plans. For example, you may want the student to be able to know what numbers come before or after a given number (lesson plans A1.4 and A1.5: Saying Next Number Word Forwards and the Next Number Word Backwards), but this skill requires that the student is able to count forwards and backwards fluently (lesson plans A1.1 and A1.2: Coping and Saying Short FNWSs or Coping and Saying Short BNWSs), so you would need to teach these skills first.

You may also want to start your teaching with some important prerequisite non-numerical skills (see Chapters 5 and 6). For example, your probe test may have revealed that your student cannot clap a given number of times (e.g., see lesson plan A6.3: Copying and Counting Monotonic Sequences of Sounds). An effective way of teaching this skill is to show (model) to the student what they need to be able to do. If the student cannot yet imitate (copy) your actions consistently, you may need to do some work on teaching imitation of movements first. It may be useful to break this skill down into simpler teaching components and gradually extend your teaching. For example, it is often easier to teach imitation of movements that involve objects first, such as copying a teacher banging on a drum or ringing a bell, before moving on to teaching imitation of large body motor movements (e.g., touching head and stomping feet). Imitation of small body movements that require fine motor actions using the hands, such as pointing or wiggling fingers, are more difficult still and you may want to teach these actions only after the student can confidently imitate behaviors from the earlier stages. Lesson plans that describe the steps for teaching imitation of motor actions can be downloaded from the website accompanying this book.

Similarly, a probe test may have revealed that a student cannot recognize and select numeral cards 1–5 when they are presented in an array on the table (e.g., see lesson plan A2.4: Numeral Recognition). An effective way to teach this skill is to hold up a picture card with the correct numeral at the same time as delivering the instruction (i.e., by using a matching prompt), for example by saying 'touch 3' at the same time as showing another card with the numeral 3. However, if the student is not yet able to match identical pictures this prompt would not be effective.

Again, this skill can be broken down into a series of easier teaching steps, for example by first teaching the student to match identical objects (e.g., placing a plastic plate on top of another plastic plate, when there are also some distractor items in the array) before moving on to teach them to match objects to corresponding pictures (e.g., matching the plastic plate to a picture of the plastic plate). Matching identical pictures (e.g., matching a photograph of the plate to another photograph) would be the next teaching step in the sequence. Lesson plans that describe the steps for teaching picture matching can be downloaded from the website accompanying this book.

Another key prerequisite skill to work on may include improving the student's general attending. If a student cannot easily orient toward teaching materials that are held up for them or laid out on the table, this may be a useful place to start teaching. It may be useful to check first that a student is able to look at reinforcing items and watch as you move the item to a variety of positions in front of them (e.g., up/down/left/right). Are they also able to do this for more common items that are less interesting to them, such as a shoe or a notebook? Lesson plans that describe the steps for teaching attending skills can be downloaded from the website accompanying this book.

Is the student likely to acquire the skill in a reasonable amount of time?

Although rates of learning can vary considerably among different children and for different skills, when you first start the numeracy program with the student it is sensible to choose your initial targets from those which the student is likely to acquire in a reasonably short amount of time. For example, if the student has a long learning history of confusing the numerals 6 and 9, you may want to leave the teaching of this skill until later when the routine of the teaching sessions is well established and they have been successful with learning some easier skills.

To use another example, if the student has limited communication skills it may take them a long time to be able to say the correct number word when shown a numeral card and to be able to articulate this in a way that can be easily understood (see lesson plan A2.5: Numeral Identification). Here, the student might be able to be taught instead to initially point to numeral cards correctly. In Chapter 4, we described how important it is that children feel as successful as possible while participating in their teaching sessions. Choosing skills at the beginning that are likely to be learnt in a reasonable amount of time is likely to be a positive experience for the student and for you as the teacher.

What impact will teaching the skill have on challenging behavior?

Sometimes children have a learning history with certain academic tasks that have contributed to challenging behavior. For example, in Chapter 1, we described how some children learn that engaging in behaviors that challenge can be very effective in keeping task demands at bay. If you know that there are certain numeracy tasks that have been problematic in the past, then try not to start teaching those until the teaching routine is well established and associated with success and high rates of reinforcement. For example, counting with one-to-one-correspondence (e.g., see lesson plan A3.1: Counting Items in One Collection) can be very difficult, and therefore aversive for some children due to their difficulty with saying the correct number word at the same time as touching the corresponding object. Always try to select initial targets to teach that you know have not previously been associated with challenging behavior. These may be easier skills to teach, or those that you know have not been taught previously.

Descriptions of the teaching activities

Now that you know where to start teaching, it is important to familiarize yourself with the teaching protocol for each target skill. These are described in detail in the lesson plans which can be downloaded from the website accompanying this book. All of the lesson plans follow the same structure. To conserve space, an example of an abbreviated lesson plan for Copying and Saying Short Forward Number Word Sequences, from the Emergent Stage, is illustrated in Figure 8.5. Most of the lesson plans when printed are between 1 and 2 pages long.

Target: A1.1 ●	Purpose: To develop knowledge of forward number word sequences in the range 1 to 20
Copying and Saying Short Forward Number Word Sequences (FNWS)	
Materials	None
Teaching procedure	Check that the student is ready to learn (looking at the teacher, sitting up straight, etc).
	Step one: Copying **For saying FNWSs *with* a modelling prompt** Teacher: 'Let's count. 1, 2, 3. Now your turn' Student: Repeats: '1, 2, 3'. Reinforce the response.
	Once mastered, continue the procedure with: • 4 to 6 • 7 to 10
	Step two: Saying **For saying FNWSs *without* a modelling prompt** Teacher: 'Count from one up to five'. Student: Says '1-2-3-4-5'. Reinforce the response.
	Once mastered, continue the procedure with: • 4 to 6 • 7 to 10
	The student should respond within 3 seconds after the instruction has been given and say the correct number sequence. If not, please refer to: Help that may be provided.

Generalization plan	• Another teacher asks the student to complete the task. • Use different instructions – e.g. 'Copy me: 1-2-3'. • Teach in a different setting or at a different time of the day.
Help that may be provided	• If the student omits a number (e.g. says 1, 2, 3, 5), the next time the sequence is modelled say the omitted number in a very loud voice, e.g. 1, 2, 3, **4** (loud), 5. • If the error continues, count backward and/or forward – for example, work on 4, 5 until consistent, then on 3, 4, 5, then on 2, 3, 4, 5, etc. • If the student continues counting on (e.g. says 1, 2, 3, 4, 5, 6... for 'count up to 5'), put up your hand to indicate when the student should stop. Alternatively, show a number card (e.g., card with the number 5) to remind them when to stop. • Each step can be introduced initially with shorter number word sequences (e.g., with two numbers), gradually building up to the longer sequences (e.g., five numbers). • If the student has difficulty pronouncing thirteen, fourteen, fifteen, etc., do some separate work where you practice working on articulation, emphasizing the part of the word they are struggling with, e.g., say, thir<u>teen.</u>
Mastering criterion	Three ticks (√) in a row across three consecutive days.

Figure 8.5 An abbreviated lesson plan for Copying and Saying Short Forward Number Word Sequences from the Emergent Stage

There are six sections to each lesson plan: (1) Target specification and learning objective; (2) Materials; (3) Teaching procedure; (4) Generalization plan; (5) Help that may be provided; and (6) Mastery criterion. These sections are described below.

Target specification and learning objective

To make it easier to refer quickly to the target that is being worked on, we developed a coding system. You will see in the lesson plan summarized in Figure 8.5, that the code for saying Short Forward Number Word Sequences is Target: A1.1.

Figure 8.6 summarizes the notation used for the lesson plans. Thus, for the lesson plan summarized above, the **A** tells us that the skill is from the Emergent Stage. The first 1 (**A1**) and the blue dot tells us that the skill is from the first key topic from that phase (in this case, Number Word Sequences from 1 to 20). The colored dot to denote the key topic helps teachers to quickly scan the printed lesson plans by color to find the key topic they are working on. The second 1 after the dot (A1.1) refers to the sequence number of the teaching activity within that key topic (i.e., it is the first teaching activity in the sequence for the Number Word Sequences key topic, which in this case happens to be Copying and Saying Short Forward Number Word Sequences).

140   Teaching Early Numeracy to Children with Developmental Disabilities

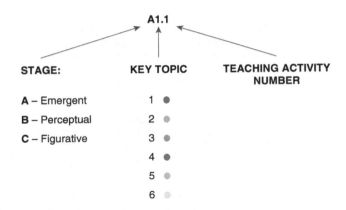

Figure 8.6 Key for deciphering target code

To use another example, B3.3: this tells us that the student is working on the third teaching activity listed under the third key topic in the Perceptual Stage (which happens to be Counting Items in Two Screened Collections from the Figurative Counting key topic). There are 94 lesson plans in *Teaching Early Numeracy to Children with Developmental Disabilities*, covering the Emergent, Perceptual and Figurative phases of mathematical development.

Materials

The materials section describes any teaching resources you may need to get ready before the teaching session, such as counters of different colors, numeral sequences (i.e., number-lines: 1–5, 1–10, 11–15, etc.), numeral tracks (numeral sequences with a small cover for each numeral), numeral cards for individual numerals, domino cards with one to six dots and cards with one to four dots in irregular patterns. The full list and description of teaching resources and a set of printable resources for *Teaching Early Numeracy to Children with Developmental Disabilities* can be downloaded from the website accompanying this book. Many of these teaching resources can be found in most school settings anyway (e.g., numeral cards, counters) but it is also relatively easy for schools to make their own resources.

Teaching procedure

The teaching procedure section of the lesson plan provides some recommendations for teaching the skill. Here, there are specifications for the instructions to use when first teaching the student and target responses you should be looking for. The teacher instructions are always highlighted in yellow so that instructors can quickly scan the lesson plan prior to teaching to find out the instruction that they should be using.

The recommended teaching procedures are generic and may need to be modified for the student you are working with. For example, as described in Chapter 7, as the student becomes more adept at using a particular skill you should be looking to vary the instructions that you use and encourage different responses from the child.

This section also provides some suggestions for breaking down skills into smaller components that may be easier for the student to learn. For example, many of the teaching procedure sections in the lesson plans have been written with the assumption that the student will initially require prompting to perform the response correctly. For example, for Saying the Number Word Before (e.g., see lesson plan A1.7) there is a specification that it might be helpful to teach the student to do this through first using a verbal imitation prompt.

Generalization plan

The generalization plan section also provides a few suggestions to encourage generalization across people or settings, stimulus generalization and sometimes some suggestions for 'teaching loosely' (see Chapter 7). However, to conserve space in the lesson plans, we included only a few suggestions in this section. Refer to Chapter 7, 'Ensuring learning lasts', for more detailed information about teaching strategies for encouraging maintenance and generalization.

Help that may be provided

The help that may be provided section summarizes some additional prompting strategies that may be helpful if a student is struggling to learn a skill. These recommendations are based on our observations of common areas of difficulty and strategies that we have observed to be useful in helping to overcome these difficulties. However, all children are different, and while some prompting suggestions are provided, there are many other prompting strategies that can be used when the student responds incorrectly or does not respond at all. Refer to Chapter 6 for more detailed information regarding prompting strategies or error correction procedures that you might find helpful.

Mastery criterion

In *Teaching Early Numeracy to Children with Developmental Disabilities*, we suggest a mastery criterion to help teachers evaluate when a student has learnt a skill. This is specified in the last section on the lesson plan. The mastery criterion refers to the number of independent correct responses over a number of days that the student needs to obtain on a target skill for that skill to be considered mastered (learnt). We have specified that the student needs to obtain one independent response (one tick) the first time they are asked to perform the target skill, across three consecutive days. This specification is described in more detail in the ongoing assessment and data collection section below.

Student's name:	Tom	Notes
Key topic 1	**A1.2 Backward Number Sequences** g. Counts backward from 5 to 1 by himself	
Data (√ or ×):	x x √ √	
Key topic 2	**A2.2 Numeral Sequences** h. 'Count forward and backward' numberlines 1–10	
Data (√ or ×):	x √ x √	
Key topic 3	**A3.2 Taking Number of Items** i. Takes 6 counters of of 30 on the table	
Data (√ or ×):	x x x √	
Key topic 4	**A4.2 Patterns in Air** h. 'Make pattern in the air' cards 1–4 flashed	Dot card used as a prompt
Data (√ or ×):	x √ x √	
Key topic 5	**A5.1 Sequential Finger Patterns** a. Raising fingers and counting 1 and 2. Child imitates	A5.1a mastered 11/14/2019
Data (√ or ×):	x √ √ √	
Key topic 6	**A6.1 Sequences** a. Copies and counts 6 chopping movements	
Data (√ or ×):	x x √ √	

Stage: Emergent

Cold Probe Data Sheet

Date: 11/11/2019

Figure 8.7   Example cold probe data sheet

Ongoing assessment and data collection

Selecting programs to teach will be an ongoing task. The student will need to be assessed prior to starting the program so that you know where to start teaching. As the student learns new skills, you will also need to know how and when to select the next appropriate goal for teaching. Data collection to monitor children's progress was described as an important component of Systematic Instruction and of our approach in Chapter 1 (see also Chapters 3 and 4). By collecting data, you will have an objective method to help you ensure that a skill is learnt and to know when to move on to the next skill to teach.

Completing a data sheet

Collecting data is an important part of this teaching approach but it should never interfere with teaching. We have selected a data collection method that is quick and easy to administer but which is also consistent with the probe test procedure described previously for your initial assessment. You should probe (test) each target the first time it is asked during the day. This is sometimes referred to as a cold probe. Any teaching effects of the previous day's session will be minimized as you are testing to see if the student has remembered the correct response the following day before any teaching has occurred. Once you have conducted the cold probe, normal teaching of the skill can resume for the rest of the session and no further data collection is required.

We consider mastery of a skill as the ability of a student to provide one independent response (one tick) the first time they are asked to perform the target skill, across three consecutive days. The children would need to demonstrate this mastery before moving on to having the next skill in the sequence assessed. It is important to probe the next skill in the sequence before you start trying to teach it as the student may demonstrate generalized responding (see Chapter 7). That is, they may be able to perform the correct response immediately without any formal teaching because of the learning that has preceded it. As with the initial assessment, if the student is correct immediately with two consecutive correct responses, the new skill can be considered known and would not need to be taught. If they score two incorrect responses, the skill should be considered not known and would need to be taught.

Cold probe data collection forms can be downloaded from the website accompanying this book and an example is provided in Figure 8.7.

The steps for completing the data sheet are described below. Examples from Figure 8.7 are illustrated in *italics*.

1. Fill in the student's name (e.g., *Tom*).
2. Fill in the developmental stage you are working on (e.g., *Emergent*). You can have more than one developmental stage if you are working on some key topics across different phases.
3. Fill in the start date for using the data collection sheet (e.g., *11 Nov 19*).

4. Fill in the code and the title of the key topic you are teaching (e.g., *A1.2 Backward Number Sequences*). The title of the topic may need to be a shorter version of the full title of the topic to fit on the form.

5. Fill in the title of the teaching activity (e.g., Counts backwards from *5 to 1 by himself*). Again, this may need to be a shorter version of the full title of the activity. You could also specify the instruction you will be using in this box.

6. Use ticks or crosses for scoring the results of your cold probe:

    *   A target is scored correct only if the student responds accurately, without help, and within three seconds.
    *   A target is scored incorrect if the student does not respond within three seconds, if they provide an incorrect response or if they require a prompt.

7. When the student scores three correct responses across three days, the skill is considered mastered (e.g., see *Sequential finger patterns* example in Figure 8.7).

8. In the note section, record any relevant information that may help your teaching in the next session (e.g., describe any helpful prompts used, *dot card used as a prompt* in the example).

9. Once the probe is completed, review your data to determine what needs to be focused on during your teaching session.

Special considerations

There may be some special considerations for data collection depending on the student and their learning history, some of which have been described elsewhere in the book. For example, if the student has a history of auditory processing difficulties (see Chapter 5) they may require more time to follow instructions than the three seconds suggested above.

The number of correct responses required for 'mastery' may also be dependent on the learning history of the child. We have suggested three independent 'cold probes' as this is a good average based on our experiences of the rate with which many children learn new skills. However, children learn at different rates. Some children may easily be able to learn a new skill within one teaching session, whereas others may take a week or even longer. If you notice that the student is usually able to respond independently by the second day of teaching, then you can reduce the cold probe requirement to correct responses over just two days. On the other hand, some children can appear to quickly forget or 'lose' mastered targets. For these children, consider increasing the number of cold probes required to reach mastery to four consecutive independent responses.

It may also be advisable to have at least two people taking the probe data to be sure that there are no instructor variables that are skewing the data. For example, one instructor may be inadvertently prompting correct responses without knowing that they are doing so (see Chapter 6).

Organizing your teaching goals

There are a few different kinds of written materials that can help you to organize your teaching. We have already described the lesson plans that provide detailed step-by-step instructions for teaching a specific skill. The cold probe data sheets will also help you structure your teaching sessions by documenting how the student is progressing with learning new skills. They generally help by providing a framework for assessing student progress so that you can ascertain if the student is learning the skills being taught in the teaching sessions. If not, teaching strategies can be modified and adapted to maximize the likelihood of each student's continued progress (see Chapters 4, 5 and 6).

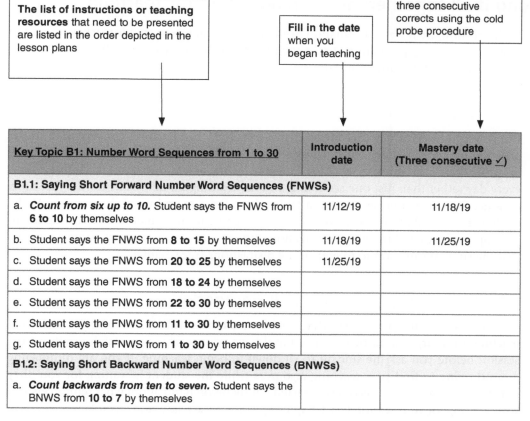

Key Topic B1: Number Word Sequences from 1 to 30	Introduction date	Mastery date (Three consecutive ✓)
B1.1: Saying Short Forward Number Word Sequences (FNWSs)		
a. *Count from six up to 10.* Student says the FNWS from **6 to 10** by themselves	11/12/19	11/18/19
b. Student says the FNWS from **8 to 15** by themselves	11/18/19	11/25/19
c. Student says the FNWS from **20 to 25** by themselves	11/25/19	
d. Student says the FNWS from **18 to 24** by themselves		
e. Student says the FNWS from **22 to 30** by themselves		
f. Student says the FNWS from **11 to 30** by themselves		
g. Student says the FNWS from **1 to 30** by themselves		
B1.2: Saying Short Backward Number Word Sequences (BNWSs)		
a. *Count backwards from ten to seven.* Student says the BNWS from **10 to 7** by themselves		

Figure 8.8 Skills tracker for Number Word Sequences from 1 to 30 in the Perceptual Stage

The following callouts point to the table above:

The list of instructions or teaching resources that need to be presented are listed in the order depicted in the lesson plans

Fill in the date when you began teaching

Fill in the date when the student achieves three consecutive corrects using the cold probe procedure

Skill trackers

Skill trackers are an additional resource that can help you keep track of the targets you should be working on. They contain crucial information such as the date when work commenced on a new skill (i.e., when it was *introduced*) and the date in which it was considered learnt (i.e., when it was *mastered*). An example of a partially completed skills tracker for key topic Number Word Sequences from 1 to 30 in the Perceptual Stage is illustrated in Figure 8.8. Blank copies of the skills tracker forms can also be downloaded from the website accompanying this book.

Teachers should refer to the skills tracker to determine which instructions to present, which teaching materials to use and which step of the program to conduct. Assuming that by reading the lesson plans, you know how to conduct your teaching for a given skill, you should have all the additional information you need, written succinctly on the skills tracker.

Putting it all together: developing a plan for teaching

In this section, we review information from previous chapters to enable teachers to start to draw up a teaching program and start their teaching. To do this, you will need to be able to answer several important questions.

Where and when should teaching happen?

Consider the time of day that the student learns best. If they are often very tired in the afternoon, try to schedule your teaching sessions for the morning. If they struggle to attend for more than a few minutes at a time, consider having at least two short teaching sessions every day rather than just one session. If you are working on new skills for the first time, conduct direct teaching sessions at a table where there are minimal disruptions. As the student acquires skills, however, transfer your teaching to more naturally occurring teaching opportunities in different generalization settings, where you can teach more loosely so that the student can learn to tolerate more distractions (see Chapter 7).

What teaching materials will be needed?

Refer to the lesson plans to see what teaching materials will be needed (if any) for the teaching of a target skill. Be organized and have your teaching materials ready for the session before you ask the student to sit down to begin teaching. If you are rummaging around trying to find your teaching resources while the student is waiting for you, they may lose their focus and become distracted. Think beforehand about what reinforcers you will be using for your session (see Chapter 4). Have these ready, and any token boards you may be using, before you start teaching.

How should I organize my teaching session?

Think about how you organize your teaching session. The first few instructions you deliver should ideally involve tasks that you know that the student is capable of performing fairly easily. Remember the 80/20 rule described in Chapter 7. The student will be more motivated if you start with easier tasks and gradually intersperse more difficult learning opportunities. It is advisable to sandwich the more difficult tasks into the middle of your teaching session so that you start and finish with easier tasks.

How can I make my lessons fun?

Remember to conduct reinforcer preference assessments before you start your teaching session so that you can be certain that the student will want to work for the items you have on offer (see Chapter 4). Try to remain animated during your sessions, delivering high rates of praise and frequent reinforcement for staying on task. Your positive feedback for correct responses should sound very different from your neutral feedback for incorrect responses (see Chapter 4). Consider having frequent breaks if the student struggles to remain on task for more than a few minutes at a time.

How will I measure the student's progress?

Ensure that you are familiar with the cold probe procedure described previously and that you know how to complete the skills tracker sheet. To increase familiarity with using the data sheets, try practicing with colleagues first before you take data on a student's responses. Remember to always bring to your teaching session any data sheets you are using to monitor progress.

What are the steps for teaching the program, and how will I know when to move on to the next teaching step?

Before you start your session, always check the data sheet from the preceding session. You will be looking in particular to see if the student needs just one more tick to master a skill. If so, look to see what the next teaching step in the sequence is in case you need to introduce this in your session. Have the teaching resources ready in case you need them. You can read the lesson plan, the probe checklists, or the skills tracker sheets for this information.

What do I do when the student responds incorrectly? How about correctly?

Be familiar with the error correction procedures described in Chapter 6. It may be helpful to role play different teaching scenarios with colleagues so that you can practice responding to errors before you work with a student. Be kind to yourself if you make mistakes. As described in Chapter 5, the teaching may feel unnatural and awkward at the beginning, but over time, as you observe how well the students are learning with this approach, you will gradually feel more at ease. For correct responses, be sure to follow the guidelines outlined in Chapters 4 and 5. Be prepared to individualize suggestions for the student you are working with. For example, while some students may respond very well to enthusiastic and animated praise, other students may require a softer and more gentle approach.

How should I encourage generalization and maintenance?

Once a new skill has been acquired, it is essential that teachers plan for maintenance and generalization (see Chapter 7). In our experience, teachers prefer to do the structured teaching at the table and sometimes do not spend enough of their teaching time ensuring that learning lasts. Use the data sheet described in Chapter 7 to plan for generalization (see Figure 7.6). The data sheet is designed in such a way that your goals can be individually determined depending on the student's home, school or community setting and the people they meet in their daily lives.

Thoughtful planning and organization of your teaching sessions should not be overlooked or assigned secondary importance. Not only will it lead to more enjoyable teaching sessions for you and the child but, crucially, it will also contribute to more successful learning outcomes for the child.

Now you are ready to use *Teaching Early Numeracy to Children with Developmental Disabilities*. Good luck!

References

Alallawi, B., Denne, L., Apanasionok, M., Grindle, C. F., & Hastings, R. (2020a). 'Special Educators' Experiences of a Numeracy Intervention for Students with Autism Spectrum Disorder': Special educators' experiences of a numeracy curriculum (TEN-DD) for students with Autism Spectrum Disorder. Manuscript submitted for publication.

Alallawi, B., Hastings, R. P., & Grindle, C, F. (2020b). Parent mediated numeracy intervention for children with Autism Spectrum Disorder in Arabic families living in the UK. Manuscript submitted for publication.

American Psychiatric Association. (2013). *Diagnostic and Statistical Manual of Mental Disorders* (5th ed.). Arlington, VA: Author.

Anderson, S. R., & Romanczyk, R. G. (1999). Early intervention for young children with autism: Continuum-based behavioural models. *Journal of the Association for Persons with Severe Handicaps*, 24, 162–73.

Apanasionok, M., Hastings, R. P., Grindle, C. F., & Alallawi, B. (2020). Teaching early numeracy to students with developmental autism using a teacher delivery model. Manuscript submitted for publication.

Ayres, K., Lowrey, K., Douglas, K., & Sievers, C. (2011). I can identify Saturn but I can't brush my teeth: What happens when the curricular focus for students with severe disabilities shifts. *Education and Training in Autism and Developmental Disabilities*, 46, 11–21.

Baer, D. M. (1999). *How to Plan for Generalization* (2nd ed.). Austin, TX: Pro-Ed.

Baer, D. M., Wolf, M. M., & Risley, T. R. (1968). Some current dimensions of Applied Behavior Analysis. *Journal of Applied Behavior Analysis*, 1, 91–7.

Baroody, A. J., Lai, M.-I., & Mix, K. S. (2006). The development of young children's number and operation sense and its implications for early childhood education. In B. Spodek & O. N. Saracho (Eds.), *Handbook of Research on the Education of Young Children* (pp. 187–221). Mahwah, NJ: Lawrence Erlbaum Associates Publishers.

Binder, C. (1996). Behavioral fluency: Evolution of a new paradigm. *Behavior Analyst*, 19, 163–97.

Bobis, J., Clarke, B., Clarke, D., Thomas, G., Wright, R. J., Young-Loveridge, J. M., & Gould, P. (2005). Supporting teachers in the development of young children's mathematical thinking: Three large scale cases. *Mathematics Education Research Journal*, 16(3), 27–57.

Browder, D. M. (2001). *Curriculum and Assessment for Students with Moderate and Severe Disabilities*. New York: Guildford Press.

Browder, D. M., & Spooner, F. (2011). *Teaching Students with Moderate and Severe Disabilities*. New York: Guilford Press.

Browder, D. M., Spooner, F., Ahlgrim-Delzell, L., Harris, A. A., & Wakeman, S. (2008). A meta-analysis on teaching mathematics to students with significant cognitive disabilities. *Exceptional Children, 74*, 407–32.

Butler, F. M., Miller, S. P., Lee, K.-H., & Pierce, T. (2001). Teaching mathematics to students with mild-to-moderate mental retardation: A review of the literature. *Mental Retardation, 39*, 20–31.

Clements, D. H., Sarama, J., & Dibiase, A. M. (2004). *Engaging Young Children in Mathematics: Standards for Early Childhood Mathematics Education*. Mahwah, NJ: Erlbaum.

Cook, B. G., & Schirmer, B. R. (2003). What is special about special education? *Journal of Special Education, 37*, 200–5.

Cook, B. G., Tankersley, M., & Landrum, T. J. (2009). Determining evidence-based practices in special education. *Exceptional Children, 75*, 365–83.

Cooper, J. O., Heron, T. E., & Heward, W. L. (2007). *Applied Behavior Analysis* (2nd ed.). Upper Saddle River, NJ: Pearson.

Department for Education. (2014). *Children with Special Educational Needs 2014: An Analysis*. Retrieved from: https://assets.publishing.service.gov.uk/government/uploads/system/uploads/attachment_data/file/350129/SFR31_2014.pdf (Accessed: 21 May 2020).

Department for Education. (2015). *Final Report of the Commission on Assessment without Levels*. London: The Stationery Office.

Department for Education. (2019). *Special Educational Needs in England: January 2019*. Retrieved from: https://assets.publishing.service.gov.uk/government/uploads/system/uploads/attachment_data/file/814244/SEN_2019_Text.docx.pdf (Accessed: 21 May 2020).

Department for Education. (2020). *Special Educational Needs: An Analysis and Summary of Data Sources*. Retrieved from: https://assets.publishing.service.gov.uk/government/uploads/system/uploads/attachment_data/file/804374/Special_educational_needs_May_19.pdf (Accessed: 21 May 2020).

Department for Education and Department of Health. (2015). *Special Educational Needs and Disability Code of Practice: 0 to 25 Years*. Retrieved from: www.gov.uk/government/publications/send-code-of-practice-0-to-25 (Accessed: 30 January 2020).

Department for Education and Department of Health. (2019). *Special Educational Needs: An Analysis and Summary of Data Sources*. Retrieved from: https://assets.publishing.service.gov.uk/government/uploads/system/uploads/attachment_data/file/804374/Special_educational_needs_May_19.pdf (Accessed: 30 January 2020).

Education Endowment Foundation. (2016). *Working with Parents to Support Children's Learning: Guidance Report*. Retrieved from: https://educationendowmentfoundation.org.uk/public/files/Publications/ParentalEngagement/EEF_Parental_Engagement_Guidance_Report.pdf (Accessed: 1 June 2020).

Education for All Handicapped Children Act of 1975, 20 U.S.C § 1401 *et seq.*

Every Student Succeeds Act. (2015). *Every Student Succeeds Act of 2015, Pub. L. No. 114-95 § 114 Stat.* 1177 (2015–2016).

Fisher, W. W., Piazza, C. C., Bowman, L. G., & Amari, A. (1996). Integrating caregiver report with a systematic choice assessment. *American Journal on Mental Retardation, 101*, 15–25.

Grobecker, B. (1999). Mathematics reform and learning disabilities. *Learning Disability Quarterly, 22*, 43–58.

Hackenberg, A. J., Norton, A., & Wright, R. J. (2016). *Developing Fractions Knowledge.* London: Sage.

Hattie, J. (2009). *Visible Learning: A Synthesis of over 800 Meta-analyses Relating to Achievement.* Abingdon and New York: Routledge.

Hayes, G. R., Hirano, S., Marcu, G. , Monibi, M., Nguyen, D. H., & Yeganyan, M.. (2010). Interactive visual supports for children with autism. *Personal and Ubiquitous Computing, 14*, 663–80.

Heward, W. L. (2003). Ten faulty notions about teaching and learning that hinder the effectiveness of special education. *The Journal of Special Education, 36*, 186–205.

Individuals with Disabilities Education Improvement Act of 2004, P.L. 108–466, 20 U.S.C. §1400, H.R. 1350.

Jimenez, B. A., Browder, D. M., & Courtade, G. R. (2008). Teaching an algebraic equation to high school students with moderate developmental disabilities. *Education and Training in Developmental Disabilities, 43*, 266–74.

Lattal, K. A., & Neef, N. A. (1996). Recent reinforcement-schedule research and applied behavior analysis. *Journal of Applied Behavior Analysis, 29*, 213–30.

Leaf, J. B., Leaf, J. A., Alcalay, A., Kassardjian, A., Tsuji, K., Dale, S., Ravid, D., Taubman, M., McEachin, J., & Leaf, R. (2016). Comparison of most-to-least prompting to flexible prompt fading for children with Autism Spectrum Disorder. *Exceptionality, 24*, 109–22.

Lee, A., Browder, D. M., Flowers, C., & Wakeman, S. (2016). Teacher evaluation of resources designed for adapting mathematics for students with significant cognitive disabilities. *Research and Practice for Persons with Severe Disabilities, 41*, 132–7.

Legislation.gov.uk. (2014). Children and Families Act 2014. Retrieved from: www.legislation.gov.uk/ukpga/2014/6/contents/enacted (Accessed: 30 January 2020).

Libby, M. E., Weiss, J. S., Bancroft, S., & Ahearn, W. H. (2008). A comparison of most-to-least and least-to-most prompting on the acquisition of solitary play skills. *Behavior Analysis in Practice, 1*, 37–43.

National Council of Teachers of Mathematics. (2000). *Principles and Standards for School Mathematics.* Reston, VA: Author.

No Child Left Behind Act of 2001, P.L. 107–110, 20 U.S.C. § 6319 (published 2002).

Oxford Learner's Dictionary. (2020). Definition of motivation. Retrieved from: www.oxford learnersdictionaries.com/definition/english/motivation (Accessed: 30 January 2020).

Pace, G. M., Ivancic, M. T., Edwards, G. L., Iwata, B. A., & Page, T. J. (1985). Assessment of stimulus preference and reinforcer value with profoundly retarded individuals. *Journal of Applied Behavior Analysis, 18,* 249–55.

Paclawskyj, T. R., & Vollmer, T. R. (1995). Reinforcer assessment for children with developmental disabilities and visual impairments. *Journal of Applied Behavior Analysis, 28,* 219–24.

Piaget, J., & Szeminska, A. (1952). *The Child's Conception of Number.* London: Routledge and Kegan Paul.

Piaget, J., Inhelder, B., & Szeminska, A. (1960). *The Child's Conception of Geometry.* London: Routledge and Kegan Paul.

Przychodzin, A. M., Marchand- Martella, N. E., Martella, R. C., & Azim, D (2004). Direct Instruction Mathematics Programs: An Overview and Research Summary, *Journal of Direct Instruction, 4,* 53–84.

Public Health England. (2015). *Learning Disabilities Observatory: People with a Learning Disability in England 2015: Main Report.* Retrieved from: www.gov.uk/government/pub lications/people-with-learning-disabilities-in-england-2015 (Accessed: 22 May, 2020).

Rizzo, K. L., & Taylor, J. C. (2016). Effects of inquiry-based instruction on science achievement for students with disabilities: An analysis of the literature. *Journal of Science Education for Students with Disabilities, 19,* 1–16.

Sands, D., Kozleski, E., & French, N. (2000). *Inclusive Education for the 21st Century.* Belmont, CA: Wadsworth/Thompson Learning.

Sarama, J., & Clements, D. (2009). *Early Childhood Mathematics Education Research.* New York: Routledge.

Skinner, B. F. (1968). *The Technology of Teaching.* New York: Appleton-Century-Crofts.

Smith, T. (2001). Discrete trial training in the treatment of autism. *Focus on Autism and Other Developmental Disabilities, 16,* 86–92.

Smith, T., Cobb, P., Farran, D., Gordray, D., Munter, C., Green, S., Garrison, A., & Dunn, A. (2010). *Evaluating math recovery: Implications for policy and practice.* Paper presented at the annual meeting of the Society for Research on Educational Effectiveness, Washington, DC.

Snyder, T. D., de Brey, C., & Dillow, S. A. (2018). *Digest of Education Statistics 2016 (NCES 2017-094).* Washington, DC: National Center for Education Statistics, Institute of Education Statistics.

Spooner, F., Root, J. R., Saunders, A. F., & Browder, D. M. (2019). An updated evidence-based practice review on teaching mathematics to students with moderate and severe developmental disabilities. *Remedial and Special Education, 40,* 150–65.

Steele, M. M. (2005). Teaching students with learning disabilities: Constructivism or behaviorism? *Current Issues in Education, 8,* 1–10.

Steffe, L. P. (1991). The constructivist teaching experiment: Illustrations and implications. In E. von Glasersfeld (Ed.), *Radical Constructivism in Mathematics Education. Mathematics Education Library,* Vol. 7. Dordrecht: Springer.

Steffe, L., & Cobb, P. (1988). *Construction of Arithmetical Meanings and Strategies.* New York: Springer-Verlag.

Stein, A., Kinder, D., Silbert, J., & Carnine, D. W. (2006). *Designing Effective Mathematics Instruction: A Direct Instruction Approach.* Upper Saddle River, NJ: Merrill/Pearson Education.

Swanson, H. L., & Sachse-Lee, C. (2000). A meta-analysis of single-subject design intervention research for students with LD. *Journal of Learning Disabilities, 33,* 114–36.

Tabor, P. D. (2018). *Math Recovery Efficacy and Effectiveness Research White Paper.* Eagan, MN: US Math Recovery Council. Retrieved from: www.mathrecovery.org/research (Accessed: 30 January 2020).

Thomas, G., & Ward, J. (2001). *An Evaluation of the Count Me In Too Pilot Project.* Available from Learning Media Customer Services, Box 3293 Wellington, NZ (Item # 10211).

Tran, L. T. (2016). *Targeted, one-to-one instruction in whole number arithmetic: A framework of key elements.* PhD thesis. Southern Cross University, Lismore, NSW.

Tryggestad, H., & Eldevik, S. (2016). Effekter av et Atferdsanalytisk Basert Program for Elever med Matematikkvansker; Et Pilotprosjekt [Effects of a behavioural analytic based program for students with mathematical difficulties: A pilot project]. *Norwegian Journal of Behavioural Analysis/Norsk Tidsskrift for Atferdsanalyse, 43,* 181–97.

Tzanakaki, P., Grindle, C. F., Saville, M., Hastings, R. P., Hughes, C. J., & Huxley, K. (2014a). An individualized curriculum to teach numeracy skills to children with autism: Program description and pilot data. *Support for Learning, 29,* 319–38.

Tzanakaki, P., Hastings, R. P., Grindle, C. F., Hughes, J. C., & Hoare, Z. (2014b). An individualized numeracy curriculum for children with intellectual disabilities: A single blind pilot randomized controlled trial. *Journal of Developmental and Physical Disabilities, 26,* 615–32.

United Nations General Assembly. (1989, November 17). *Adoption of a Convention on the Rights of the Child.* New York: United Nations.

United Nations General Assembly. (2006). *Convention on the Rights of Persons with Disabilities: Resolution / adopted by the General Assembly,* 24 January 2007, A/RES/61/106. Retrieved from: www.refworld.org/docid/45f973632.html (Accessed: 30 January 2020).

Vaughn, S., & Dammann, J. D. (2001). Science and sanity in special education. *Behavioral Disorders, 27,* 21–9.

von Glasersfeld, E. (1984). An introduction to radical constructivism. In P. Watzlawick (Ed.), *The Invented Reality.* New York: Norton, pp. 17–40.

von Glasersfeld, E. (Ed.) (1991). *Radical Constructivism in Mathematics Education. Mathematics Education Library,* Vol. 7. Dordrecht: Springer.

Westling, D. L., & Fox, L. (2004). *Teaching Students with Severe Disabilities* (3rd ed.). Upper Saddle River, NJ: Pearson/Merrill/Prentice Hall.

Willey, R., Holliday, A., & Martland, J. (2007). Achieving new heights in Cumbria: Raising standards in early numeracy through mathematics recovery. *Educational & Child Psychology, 24,* 108–18.

Wright, R. J. (2003). A mathematics recovery: Program of intervention in early number learning. *Australian Journal of Learning Difficulties, 8*(4), 6–11.

Wright, R. J., Cowper, M., Stafford, A., Stanger, G., & Stewart, R. (1994). *The Mathematics Recovery project – a progress report: Specialist teachers working with low-attaining first-graders.* Paper presented at the 17th annual conference of the Mathematics Education Research Group of Australia.

Wright, R. J., & Ellemor-Collins, D. (2018). *The Learning Framework in Number: Pedagogical Tools for Assessment and Instruction.* London: Sage.

Wright, R. J., Ellemor-Collins, D., & Tabor, P. (2012). *Developing Number Knowledge: Assessment, Teaching and Intervention with 7–11 Year-Olds.* London: Sage.

Wright, R. J., Martland, J., & Stafford, A. K. (2006a). *Early Numeracy: Assessment for Teaching and Intervention,* 2nd edition. London: Sage.

Wright, R. J., Martland, J., Stafford, A. K., & Stanger, G. (2006b). *Teaching Number: Advancing Children's Skills and Strategies,* 2nd edition. London: Sage.

Wright, R. J., Stanger, C., Stafford, A. K., & Martland, J. (2014). *Teaching Number in the Classroom with 4–8 Year-Olds,* 2nd edition. London: Sage.

Index

Page numbers in *italics* refer to figures; page numbers in **bold** refer to tables.